cover and frontispiece
Methuen, C.1900 corner of
Broadway and Osgood Sts. looking north

Methuen c.1900, corner of Broadway and
Osgood Sts. looking north

A History
of
the Town of
Methuen

by
Joseph S. Howe

preface by
Stephen N. Zanni
Mayor of Methuen

SicPress.com 2012
Methuen, MA

"Town of Methuen" previously appeared in Volume II of History of Essex County, Massachusetts with biographical sketches of many of its pioneers and prominent men, edited by D. Hamilton Hurd, published in 1888, by J. W. Lewis & Co.

edited by J. Godsey
for copies sales@SicPress.com
Methuen, MA 2012

Table of Contents

PREFACE

While so much attention is paid to historical events from around the world, too often we overlook the impact that local history has in shaping the communities in which we live in. In fact, it is one of the great ironies that preserving local history is both incredibly easy, and yet at the same time incredibly difficult.

The City of Methuen we know today is rich in both history and culture. With almost 50,000 residents, Methuen possesses urban, suburban and rural settings. A feeling that is unique among modern communities, Methuen is a city that at times can feel so large, and at other times feels like a small, New England town. Understanding where Methuen is today would not be possible without understanding our City's exciting history.

Local history is the story most easily within reach. Artifacts and architecture both are at the disposal of any interested party. Yet when it comes to preserving local history, too often the onus is placed on volunteers. As municipalities are under constant pressure to cut costs, a sad reality is that historical preservation is many times considered a luxury that cannot be afforded. As local governments pull back and volunteers come and go, memories can fade and stories can be lost.

Take pride in your local history, and appreciate the hard work that was put into these very pages. This book offers our residents, now and in the future, the opportunity to see the history that is Methuen.

Mayor Stephen N. Zanni

Geography.

The town of Methuen is situated in the westerly part of Essex County, bordering on New Hampshire and contains within its limits about twenty-two square miles.

Before the incorporation of the City of Lawrence, it was a section of land on the north bank of the Merrimack River about nine miles long and three miles wide, following the curves of the river.

The north part of the City of Lawrence was taken out of the middle of the town, thus leaving the two ends three miles wide, and the middle of the town little more than a mile at its narrowest part.

The towns surrounding Methuen are the City of Lawrence and the town of Andover on the South, Dracut, and Salem, N.H. on the West, Salem, N.H., and Haverhill, on the North and Haverhill and Bradford on the East.

The Spicket River, a narrow and crooked stream, flows from Island Pond in Derry, N.H. through Methuen, into Lawrence and empties into the Merrimack in the lower part of the city. The village of Methuen is situated upon both sides of the Spicket, between Lawrence and the New Hampshire line, thus dividing the farming portions of the town into two not unequal sections. The surface of the town is uneven, somewhat hilly and picturesque, though not ledge and abrupt. The soil in the main is strong, and good for ordinary agriculture, but like most New

England land, more of less rock, requiring much labor to insure agricultural success, but capable of producing excellent crops under judicious management.

There is a strip of intervale land of varying width on the bank of the Merrimack, free from stone, easy to cultivate and excellent for farming purposes. Leaving this level intervale, the land rises into ridges and hills, much of it covered with a growth of wood. There are extensive peat meadows in both sections of the town, which not only contain large quantities of alleged fuel, but, when drained and cultivated, prove to be the most valuable lands for the production of many crops.

The hill formerly known as "Bare Hill," near the house of Joel Foster, is the highest elevation in the east part of the town, and affords a magnificent view of the country in every direction for miles around. As many as fifteen towns and cities may be seen from its summit. It overlooks Lawrence on the south, with the two Andovers beyond, and the spires of Haverhill and Bradford may be seen on the East. Far off to the North can be seen the Nottingham Hills, and in the West the Uncanoonucks, the Peterboro Hills, Monadnock and Wachuset, "Like giant emeralds in the Western sky." The view, besides being extensive, is one of the most beautiful to be found. In the west part of the town, the highest land is on the hill, which is the residence of Stephen W. Williams, Esq.

The view from its top is nearly as extensive, and quite as beautiful, as that from Bare Hill, and it is a favorite resort for lovers of fine scenery.

The ponds in Methuen are few in number; Harris Pond, in the extreme west part of the town, contains about fifty acres, and drains through "London Meadow" into Spicket River. Mystic Pond, a little west of Methuen drains into Spicket River. World's End Pond, a mile or more north of Methuen village, lies mostly in Salem, N.H., although a very small part of it is within the limits of Methuen, and drains into the Spicket.

10

There is also a small pond in Strong Water Meadow, known as "Strong Water Pond," which is undoubtedly a small remnant of what was once a large body of water. Bloody Brook runs from Strong Water Meadow southerly into Lawrence and empties into the Spicket. Hawkes Brook is in the extreme northerly part of the town rising near Ayers village, in Haverhill, and emptying into the Merrimack, where Methuen and Haverhill join. Barlett Brook, in the west part of Methuen, runs from Mud Pond in Dracut, into Methuen, and empties into the Merrimack.

There are no stone quarries or ledges that are worked in the town. A bed of secondary rock for the most park underlies the town a short distance below the surface, and crops out in a few places, particularly in the neighborhood of the village, but the quality of the stone is not such as to make it specially valuable for building purposes. The rocks found in the soil, and on the surface of the land, are mainly boulders, many of them primary rock, and nearly all of a different kind of stone from the underlying ledge, indicating that the mass of gravel and stones, resting upon the ledge, has been brought there from a distance by glacial action.

There are in Methuen some very marked examples of glacial action in the ridges known to geologists as "Kames," and to the unscientific as "Hogbacks." One of these ridges extends from Tower Hill, in Lawrence, through the west part of Methuen village into New Hampshire, and is a continuation of the series of "Kames" running through Andover and Reading, and known in Andover as "Indian Ridge." There is also another line of "Kames," extending from the easterly part of the City of Lawrence through "Germantown" northward. In the early times, these ridges were thought by many to be the remains of ancient fortifications, but the investigations of geologists have determined, beyond question, that they were deposits formed in the melting ice.

Methuen contains few natural objects of special interest, Spicket Falls being perhaps the most prominent. The Nevins Memorial, and grounds of Henry C. Nevins, near by, and the extensive grounds of Chas. H. Tenney, are beautifully laid out and kept, contain many rare and costly trees and shrubs, and are all places which would attract attention anywhere.

When the country first became known to the white race, the hills and uplands were mainly covered by a heavy growth of timber. The meadows were mostly cleared and covered with a thick, heavy growth of grass, which the Indians were accustomed to burn in the autumn. These meadows were favorite haunts of deer, which came there to feed on the young grass in the spring, and could easily be killed by the Indians from their hiding-places on the wooded bushy edges. It is said that some of the hills were bare, and others had only growth of small wood. This would naturally result from the fires set by the Indians in dry weather, which might spread from the meadows to the upland, and kill the standing wood and timber. It would also appear that the Indians cultivated corn to some extent, and from that, purpose selected the lands free from stones, easily worked on the river intervales and sandy plains. We can easily imagine the appearance of this town as the earliest settlers saw it:

The meadows on Hawke's Brook, in the east part of the town: Bare meadow, Strong meadow, Mystic meadows, London meadows, and the meadows on the banks of the Spicket, mostly bare, and producing a heavy crop of grass. The intervale land on the Merrimack, more and less cleared, and a few spots of plan land here and there, barren of trees and grass, and bearing the marks of the rude Indian agriculture, the rest of the lands covered with wood and timber. The only paths traversing this wilderness were Indian trails, of whose location we have now no knowledge, though it is not unlikely that some of our oldest roads were developed from an Indian path.

ORIGINAL INHABITANTS.

The earliest settlers found very few Indians living in this vicinity. Some years before the first settlement of this country, a violent war broke out among the Indians living in what is now New England, which resulted in the destruction of a large number. This was followed by a pestilence, which carried off many more, and was especially fatal in the eastern part of New England. This destruction of the Indians was particularly favorable to the occupation of the country by the white settlers. The native inhabitants of the valley of the Merrimack, so far as we know, were the Pennacooks or Pawteucket Indians. These were subdivided into smaller tribes or families. The Agawams had their home on the coast from the Merrimack to Cape Ann; the Wamesits, at the junction of the Concord and Merrimack Rivers, where Lowell now stands; the Pawtuckets, at the mouth of the Little River in Haverhill.

No historic evidence appears that any Indian tribe had a permanent home in Methuen, but it is known that Bodwell's Falls (at the Lawrence dam), the region around the mouth of Bartlett's Brook, and the shores of the Spicket, as far as Spicket Falls, were favorite resorts of the Indians, especially during the fishing season. There are also strong indications that there were once permanent Indian settlements near Spicket Falls and near the mouth of London Brook. The stone fire-places or hearths of their wigwams were found years ago, before the ground was disturbed, on the hillside where the east part of Methuen village is now built. Arrow-points, spear-heads and other Indian relics were found while digging the cellars of Woodbury's Block, the hotel stable and in other places. A large stone pot was discovered while excavating for the foundation of Tenney's hat-shop and the Indian grave was found in the fall of 1886, while digging Union Street, which contained eight very fine spear-heads, be-

13

sides arrow-heads and pottery, indicating that the occupant of the grave was a person of distinction. The early records of Haverhill speak of an old wigwam near the "foot of far west meadow," which was probably what is now known as "London Meadow." The Indian fire-places can be found there now, where the land has not been cultivated and stones disturbed. These old hearths and graces would seem to show that the spots where they are found were at some time the sites of permanent Indian villages and not merely a transient place of abode for a few weeks while fishing.

The rivers in those early times swamped with alewives, shad, salmon, bass, and sturgeon. The salmon was the principal fish used as food, and the shad and alewives were used by the Indians to manure their corn. These fish were caught by them around the falls and rapids in the rivers. It would be natural, therefore, for them to settle about such a spot as Spicket Falls, which must have afforded an excellent fishing-place, while the land south and east of the falls was easy for them to cultivate for corn. The neighborhood for London Brook and Policy Brook—up which the alewives and suckers must have run in great numbers—would also have been an excellent place for an Indian village, particularly as there was plenty of land easy to work near-by.

Probably the white man first set foot in Methuen about two hundred and fifty year ago. The settlers at Ipswich and other towns along the coast explored the country before its settlement to find the most desirable places to locate. In 1640 about a dozen colonists from Newbury, headed by Mr. Nathaniel Ward, settled at Haverhill, where the city proper now stands. Two years later, they purchased from the Indians a tract of land embracing the greater part of what is now Methuen. The original deed is now in possession of the city of Haverhill, and reads as follows:

KNOW ALL MEN BY THESE PRESENTS, that we, Passaquo and Saggahew, with ye consent of Passaconnaway: have sold unto ye in-

14

habitants of Pentuckett all ye lands we have in Pentuckett; that is eyght myles in length from ye little Rivver in Pentuckett Westward; Six myles in length from ye aforesaid Rivver northward; And six myles in length from ye foresaid Rivver Eastward, with ye Ileand and ye rivver that ye ileand stand in as far in length as ye land lyes by as formerly expressed: that is fourteen myles in length;

And wee ye said Passaquo and Sagga Hew with ye consent of Passaconnaway, have sold unto ye said inhabitants all ye right that wee or any of us have in ye said ground and Ileand and Rivver;

And we warrant it against all or any other Indians whatsoever unto ye said Inhabitants of Pentuckett, and to their heirs and as signs forever. Dated ye fifteenth day of November Ann Dom 1642. Witness our hands and scales to this bargayne of sale ye day and year above written (in ye presents of us) we ye said Passaquo & Sagga Hew have received in hand, for & in consideration of ye same three pounds & ten shillings.

John Ward
Robert Clements
Tristan Coffin
Hugh Sherratt
William White
Thomas Davis

Passaquo, a mark of a box and arrow
Saggahew, a mark of a box and arrow

It is not easy to determine exactly what the Indians intended to convey by this deed, nor does it appear to have been clear to the early settlers. No regular survey was made until 1666, when a committee was appointed by the General Court to "run the bounds of the Town of Haverhill." They began at the meeting-house which was situated about half a mile east of Little River, near the cemeteries in the eastern part of the present city of Haverhill, and ran due west eight miles, and "reared a heap of stones." Then they ran from the heap of stones due south until they reached the Merrimac River and due north from the heap of stones until they struck the northern line of the town. The shape of Haverhill, as finally determined, was triangular. Starting from Holt's Rock (Rocks Village), the line ran due northwest until it met the north and south line from Merrimac River, as mentioned above. There is an old plan in the County Records, made previously to 1700, and probably as early as 1675, from which it appears that the Haverhill line started from the little island in the Merrimac, situated nearly opposite the junction of Lowell and North Lowell Streets. From thence the line ran due north, very near the house of A. W. Pinney, across from Policy Pond, and struck the Haverhill north line, northwest of Island Pond, including most, if not all, of that fine sheet of water withing the limits of Haverhill. Thus, it appears that the title to all that portion of Methuen east of above-described line, came directly from the aboriginal owners.

EARLY SETTLERS.

It is noticeable that the Indian deed conveyed the river and the islands in it, and thus that Haverhill and Methuen are bounded by the opposite shore of the Merrimac, instead of the center or channel. It will also be noticed that this land was conveyed to "ye inhabitants to Pentuckett." and consequently was owned by the inhabitants of the town or colony in common. Here was an example of the common ownership of land by a community, the practical working of which is interesting to follow now, when so many reformers are holding forth the idea that such ownership of the land would be the chief remedy for the evils of modern civilization. But the early settlers were evidently not possessed with the idea that this would be good for them, and did not long cultivate the land in this way, but took steps to let every man have his own land in severalty. The records of the town of Haverhill show that no one was admitted to the rights and privileges of the colony unless first voted in by the town.

In 1643, it was voted that

There shall be three hundred acres laid out for house lotts[sic] and no more; and that he that was worth two hundred pounds should have

16

twenty acres to his house lott, and none to exceed that number; and so every one under that sum, to have acres proportionable to his house lott, together with meadow and common and planting ground, proportionably.

The site of these "house lotts" was where the city proper of Haverhill now stands, a short distance east from Little River. Here all the colonists had their houses, from which, as a center, they sought out the meadows and planting grounds in the more distant part of the town. The meadow-lands seem to have been the most highly valued, and sought after on account of the grass, which was the principal subsistence for their cattle. They cut and stacked the hay in the summer, and in the winter drew it home in sleds. The planting grounds were probably patches of upland, which had been cultivated by the Indians, and were free from trees. An early writer says of Haverhill:

> The people are wholly bent to improve their labor in tilling the earth and keeping of cattel[sic] whose yearly increase encourages them to spend their days in those remote parts. The constant penetrating further into this WIlderness hath caused the wild and uncouth woods to be filled with frequented wayes, and the large rivers to be overlaid with Bridges passeable both for horse and foot; this Town is of large extent, supposed to be ten miles in length, there being an overweaning desire in most men after Meadow-land, which hath caused many towns to grasp more into their hands than they could afterward possibly hold.

Lot layers were chosen by the town to divide the meadows and planting-grounds among the inhabitants, from time to time, as these lands became accessible and in a condition to cultivate. The records of these divisions show that the lots set off at first were small, often not more than two or three acres in a lot, and the meadow-land seems to have been taken up first. So it happened that a man would own lots in the eastern part of Haverhill, and on Spicket River and might be obliged to travel several miles to his planting-ground in another direction. The distribution of land went on from year to year, and the natural result was that land-owners desiring to have their lands as much as possible in one body, traded with each other until they became possessed of a compact body of land sufficient for a farm. The next step was to build and settle on the farm for greater economy and convenience in cultivation of the land, and so the settlers gradually scattered from the first compact settlements out over the town. The descriptions of the lots as set off by the lot layers are recorded in the Haverhill records, but it is very difficult to exactly locate them now, because the bounds were usually marked trees, stumps and other perishable monuments.

These old descriptions show, however, that some of our local names are of very ancient date. In 1658, five acres of meadow were laid off in "Strongwater," near a little pond. In 1666, a parcel of meadow was laid out to Matthias Button, on the south side of "Spicket Hill." In 1659, there was a division of the land west of the Spicket River, with a provision that "if more than two acres meadow be found on any one lot, it shall remain to the town." In the same year, we find a record of the laying off three acres of land in "Mistake Meadow" in the western part of Haverhill, whence we may fairly conclude that our present name "Mystic," was once "Mistake." In 1678 "eleven score acres of upland" were laid off to James Davis, Sr., bounded on the west by Spicket River, Spicket Falls being the southwest bound. In 1683 we find that a lot adjoining, on the southerly side, running from Spicket Falls to "Bloody Brook" on the east was taken up by James Davis, Jr. These two lots included the land now occupied by the east part of Methuen village. The family of Mr. David Nevins, have in their possession a grant from the "proprietors" of the Islands in the Spicket above the falls, to Asa and Robert Swan, for two pounds ten shillings, and bearing the date of 1731.

The distribution of the common lands was continued between the town, and they disposed of the remaining land as they saw fit. This is appears that the titles to the land in Methuen, east of the old Haverhill line, have all come from the Indians, Passaquo and Saggahew, through the "proprietors." The strip of land in Methuen, perhaps a mile and a half in width, between Haverhill line and "Dawcut" or Dracut line, seems to have been granted by the General Court to individuals. Major Denison, who had a grant of six hundred acres from the General Court in 1660, owned more than a thousand acres on the river above the Haverhill line, including what is now known as the Bartlett farm, and lands south and west. West of that was Colonel Higginson's farm of over three hundred acres. A little north of these was Marshall Nicholson's tract of three hundred acres. Printer Green had three hundred acres lying on each side of the brook, which runs from "White's Pond," then called "North Pond."

As we have already stated, we can find no record showing when the first settlement was made within the present limits of Methuen, or who made it.

It is certain that the east and south parts of the town near the river, were first occupied, doubtless because they were nearer the villages of Haverhill and Andover. It is said that when repairing the old "Bodwell House" now in Lawrence, some years ago, a brick was found bearing the date 1660, which had been marked upon it before the brick was burnt. This would seem to indicate that a house was built in the neighborhood near that date. It seems doubtful whether there were many settlers in Methuen until near the time it was set off from Haverhill. The Indian troubles which, extended over many years previous to 1700, must have seriously checked, if they did not entirely prevent, the settlement on farms. Andover and Haverhill were both made frontier towns by act of General Court, and both towns suffered severely during the Indian attack on settlers living upon territory which, afterwards became Methuen. There were many attacks on the scattered settlers in West Haverhill and in Andover, and if there had been many inhabitants in Methuen, it is hardly probable that the Indians would have passed them by. The incursions of the Indians seem to have come sometime, from the North, by way of Dover and Saco; and sometimes from the West, down the Merrimack valley; as was the case when Hannah Duston was taken captive; and sometimes the depredations were committed by small parties of Indians, who had lived among the whites and were acquainted with their victims. In February 1698, Jonathan Haynes and Samuel Ladd, with their sons, had been to London Meadow from their homes in West Haverhill for hay each with a team consisting of a pair of oxen and a horse. The path lay along between World's End Pond and what is now Howe Street. When returning home, just northeast of the pond, they were suddenly attacked by a party of Indians who had concealed themselves in the bushes on each side of the parth. These Indians, fourteen in number, were returning from Andover, where they had killed and captured several persons. They killed Haynes and Ladd with their hatchets took one of the boys prisoner and kept him for some years; the other boy cut one of the horses loose, jumped on his back, and got away. The Indians then killed the oxen, took out the tongues and best pieces, and went on their way. This is the only authentic instance we can find of an Indian outrage happening on Methuen soil.

HAVERHILL PARTITION.

In 1712 nine persons living in that part of Haverhill which is now Methuen, petitioned the town to abate their rates for the support of the ministry and the schools, "on account of the great distance they lived from the town, and the difficulty they met with in coming," and the town voted to abate one-half the ministry rates.

The names of these persons were Henry Bodwell, John Gutterson, Thomas Austin, Joshua Stephens, Robert Swan, John Cross, William Cross, Robert Swan, Jr. Joshua Swan.

In July 1719, a petition was presented to the Town of Haverhill by Stephen Barker, Henry Bodwell and others "to grant or set them off a certain tract of land lying in the township of Haverhill, that so they might be a township or parish, but this request was denied.

At the next March meeting, the following petition was presented:

Whereas there is a certain tract of land in the west end of Haverhill containing fifty or sixty acres, lying on the south and southwest of a meadow a meadow commonly called bare meadow, which land, together with a piece of land lying on a hill called meeting-house hill, in times passed reserved by our forefathers for the use of the ministry, might in hard times make a convenient parsonage; if by the blessing of God, the gospel might so flourish amongst us, and we grow so populous as to be able to carry on the gospel ministry amongst us. We therefore humbly pray that you would take into consideration the circumstances we are in, and the difficulty we may hereafter meet with in procuring a privilege for the ministry; and that you would grant and settle and record the above said lands in your Town book, for the above said use, and you will gratify your humble petitioners and oblige us and our posterity to serve you hereafter in what we may.

This petition was signed by Joshua Swan and twenty-six others, "was granted according to the proposals therein made," and in July following, a committee was chosen to lay out the land.

It seems, from this petition, that the proprietors of the common land had some time previously "reserved for the use of the ministry" two tracts of land in what was afterwards Methuen, but that this land had not been formally laid out. In 1724 Lieutenant Stephen Barker and other inhabitants of the western part of Haverhill, petitioned the General Court for a new town, to be formed by setting off that part of Haverhill above Hawke's Meadow Brook.

The town of Haverhill voted to oppose the petition, and chose Captain John White agent for that purpose. Opposition however was unavailing, and the act was passed December 8, 1725, and was as follows:

AN ACT for Dividing the Town of Haverhill and erecting a new Town there, and in parts adjacent, by the name of Methuen. Where as the

21

West part of the Town of Haverhill within the County of Essex, and parts adjacent not included within any Township is Competently filled with Inhabitants, who labor under great Difficulties by their remoteness from the place of Publick Worship, &c., and they having made their application to this Court that they may be set off a distinct and separate Town and be vested with all the Powers and Privileges of a Town. Be it therefore enacted by the Lieutenant Governor, Council and Representatives in General Court assembled and by the authority of the same. That the West part of the said Town of Haverhill with the laud adjoining be, and hereby are set off and constituted a separate Township by the name of Methuen, the bounds of the said Township to be as follows, viz—: Beginning at the month of Hawkes Meadow Brook, so called, in Merrimack River, and from thence to run half a point to the north ward of the northwest to an heap of stories, or till it intersect Hav erhill line; from thence upon a straight course to the head of Dunstable line, and so upon Dracut line about four miles to a pine southeast, frome thence six miles or thereabouts upon Dracut line, South to Merrimack River, and from thence to run down said river ten mile and forty pole till it come to the first mentioned bounds. And that "the inhabitants of the said lands as before described and bounded, be and hereby are invested with the Powers, Privileges and Immunities that the Inhabitants of any of the towns of this Province by law are or ought to be vested with.

Provided, That the Inhabitants of the said Town of Methuen, do within the space of Three Years from the Publication of this Act erect and finish a suitable house for the Publick Worship of God, and procure and settle a Learned, Orthodox minister of good conversation and make provision for his comfortable and honorable support, and that they set apart a lot of Two Hundred acres of land in some convenient Place in the said Town, for the use of the ministry, and a lot of fifty acres for the use of a School. And that thereupon they be discharged from any further payments for the maintenance of the ministry in Haverhill. And be it further enacted by the authority aforesaid, That the Inhabitants of the said Town of Methuen, be and hereby are empowered to assess all the lands of Non residents lying within the said town, Two pence per acre towards the building of the Meeting House, and settling of a minister there. Provided, nevertheless that there be and here by is made a Reservation or Saving of the Right and property of the Province Lands (if any there be) within the bounds aforesaid, to this Province.

INCORPORATION.

So far as we can learn, no other town in the country bears the name of *"Methuen."* How this name originated has been a matter of considerable speculation. Some have thought that it took its name from a town in Scotland called "Methven," and others have supposed that this town was named in honor of Lord Methven of Scotland. A. C. Goodell, Esq., of Salem, who is engaged in preparing the Provincial Laws for publication, suggests a theory which we think must be the true one. It was a common thing in those days, when a town was incorporated, for the Governor to give it a name. The act of incorporation was passed by the Legislature, engrossed and sent to the Governor, for his signature, with a space for the name of the new town in blank. When he signed the act, he gave the town its name and inserted it in the proper place. The original act of incorporation of the Town of Methuen, in the office of the Secretary of State, clearly shows that the name was inserted by a hand different from the one that engrossed the bill. The act is written upon the parchment in a large, full hand, while the name *"Methuen"* is written in a small, running hand, and with ink of a different color, but similar to that used by Governor Dummer, in writing his signature. Had the name been suggested by the petitioners for the act of incorporation, it would have been likely to be inserted in the bill and so copied by the engrossing clerk. But, a careful examination of the writing leaves little doubt that Governor Dummer wrote the name with his own hand, when he attached his signature. Of course, it is now impossible to ascertain with certainty the reason, which suggested the name to him. But, at that time there was one Lord Paul Methuen, who was Privy Councillor to the Kind, and who was for some years likely that Governor Dummer was a personal or political

23

friend and admirer of this nobleman, and so name the town in his honor.

The town of Methuen, as originally set off, must have included more than double the territory now within its limits. Starting from the mouth of Hawke's Meadow Brook, the line ran where it now does through Ayers Village, and continued on until it met the west line of Haverhill, which must have been somewhere southwest of North Salem Village; thence it ran straight to the "head of Dunstable line," which was in Pelham, "in sight of Beaver Brook," and a little to the west of it; thence it ran southeast about four miles to Dracut line, at a point about six miles from Merrimack River. The easterly line of Dracut has not been materially changed, and therefore the present line, prolonged to six miles, would indicate the old corner of that town. The old plan in the County Records, already referred to, shows that this corner was west of Policy Pond, and must have been in the vicinity of "Spear Hill," almost between the most southern parts of Policy and Cobbett's Ponds. From this it would seem that Methuen, as originally incorporated, included nearly all of Salem, Windham village and perhaps two-thirds of that town, and a little of Pelham. Cobbett's Pond and Policy Pond were both in Methuen. The old plan referred to gives the name of Policy Pond as "Poliss's Pond," which fact may possibly furnish clue to the origin of the name "Policy." The lands in the westerly part of Methuen were evidently disputed territory.

Londonderry, settled by the "Scotch-Irish," was incorporated, in 1722, by the General Court of New Hampshire, and the act of incorporating the town included quite a slice of land set off to Methuen by the Massachusetts General Court. It is probable, however, that the territory claimed under both acts was not much settled upon, or considered of much value, until after the line between Massachusetts and New Hampshire was established in 1740.

To organize the new town, it was ordered by the Court

24

that Mr. Stephen Barker, a principal inhabitant of the Town of Methuen, be and hereby is empowered and directed to notifie[sic] and summons the inhabitants of the said town, duly qualified for voters, to assemble and meet sometime in the month of March next, to choose town officers according to law to stand for the year.

In compliance with this order, a meeting was appointed for the 9th of March, 1726.

Att our first annual meeting in the town of methueu, march ye 9th 1725, 6 Leutanent Stephen Barker was leaguly chosen moderator for ye meeting.

Att the same meeting william whittier was chosen town clark & sworn for ye yer insewing.

Att the same meeting selectmen war leaguly chosen for ye year.
1 John Bailey,
2 Ebenezer Barker
3 Asie Swan
4 Daniel Bodwel
5 Thomas Whittier

Att ye same meeting Richard swan is leaguly chosen cunstable for the year iusewing.

Voted that the cunstable or colector shall be paid one shilling for each twenty shillings of money that he shall colect or gather of the Taxes which shall be laied upon the nonrazedance or peopel which belong to other towns. March ye 9th 1725,6 the toun voted that Thomas silver should be excepted to serve cunstable or colector instead of Richard swan for ye year insewing and ye same day thomas silver was sworn to the fathfull discharge of the office of a cunstable by the selectmen of methuen. Robert swan is leaguly chosen town treasurer att the same meeting march ye 9 for ye year insewing. town treasurer sworn.[sic]

Att ye same meeting march ye 9 voted yt hogs should go att large acording to law.

Att a town meeting march ye 9 1725,6,

Voted that the selectmen should have "athadoxt minester"[sic] to serve in the work of insewing and not to exceed five and forty pownds minester his diat.[sic]

The records of the town-meetings held since that time appear to be complete, and the early records quite as full as such records usually are. The first business done by the new Board of Selectmen was to lay out a road "three rods wide, beginning at a white oak tree marked, near Ephraim Clark's and; from thence across Thomas Eaton's, and by the west side of Samuel Clark's cellar; thence by the west side of a white oak marked with H by Hawks' meadow, and so along said meadow, as near as it convenient, to the lower end, crossing the brook between two maple trees marked; from thence, as the trees are marked, to a white oak by Haverhill path, running from the east side of the tree in the path until we come to a stake by James How's well, and thence to a white oak marked with H, the way being to the east." This was undoubtedly the road north of the Taylor farm, on Howe Street and the above description is a good example of the recorded descriptions of the ancient ways. The records of the town of Haverhill show that previous to this time a large number of town-ways had been laid out in the west part of the town, probably for convenience in reaching the meadows and woodland. At this distance of time, it is almost impossible to trace them unless they happen to touch some well-known point. They generally commence at a marked tree by some path, thence to some other tree, thence to a stump marked, and finally come out at another path, and are almost invariably two rods wide.

The roads of those days were probably little better than an ordinary cart-path in the woods. Occasionally we find a record of money paid to the owners of land over which a public way passed, but no money appears to have been paid to the town for building.

In fact, scarcely more than a path was necessary, for there were no vehicles but ox-carts and sleds. People traveled on horseback, and went to market with their goods in saddle-bags. Persons are now living in the town who say they can remember when there were no wagons of any kind, or pleasure carriages, except a few chaises, which were introduced about the beginning of the century.

The First Meeting-house.

On the 14th of June 1726, the second town-meeting was called at the house of Asie Swan, "to prefix a place whereon to build a meeting-house" and make other necessary arrangements for religious service. At this meeting, a bitter controversy began about the location of the meeting-house. Votes being called for, the following persons voted for "a place between James Davis' and Samuel Smith's house," supposed to be on what is now known as "Powder-House Hill:"

John Hastings	Thomas Whittier
Samuel Clark	Samuel Currier
John Messer	Robert Swan
Daniel Lancaster	Ephraim Clark
Thomas Messer	James Emery
Robert Corgill	Joseph Pudney
Samuel Smith	John Rue
John Cross	Asie Swan
William Cross	James How
John Bailey	Abraham Masters
Richard Messer	James Wilson
Thomas Silver	Abiel Messer
Nathaniel Messer	Daniel Peaslee
Thomas Eaton	Richard Swan

The following persons entered their dissent against the meeting-house being carried from the meeting-house land or hill, –

Stephen Barker	Joseph Morse
Henry Bodwell	Henry Bodwell, Jr.
John Gutterson	Daniel Bodwell

Samuel Huse	Joseph Gutterson
James Bodwell	Zebediah Barker
John Harris	Thomas Austin
William Gutterson	Thomas Richardson
Benjamin Stevens	Abel Merrill
James Barker	Ebenezer Barker
Samuel Stevens	Joshua Swan
Zebediah Austin	

It is likely that these two lists comprise the names of about all the persons entitled to vote then living in Methuen. We infer also that this dispute was one concerning convenience of access to the meeting-house, and that the voters cast their ballots for the location that was nearest or would best accommodate them.

On the 26th of August, another meeting was called to prefect the arrangements for building the new meeting-house. It was voted that the meeting-house should be built forty-feet long, thirty-five feet in width and twenty feet stud.

It was also voted to choose a committee to procure land to set the meeting house on, to provide timber and hire a carpenter and other workmen, and provide for the raising, "all upon the town's cost and charge." The meeting then adjourned to meet September 6th. At this meeting the dissenters above named presented the following quaint and vigorous protest, —

We, the subscribers, dissent against the proceedings pursuant to sundry of the particulars as mentioned in the warrant for the meeting,

First, for that in the warrant, the day being prefixed, but the year is not.

2. For the bigness of the meeting-house according to the warrant, to this we dissent, for the bigness cannot be known until a committee be chosen and bound out the land, for the particulars being placed in the warrant agreeably to the old saying 'the cart before the horse,' therefore irregular.

3. To choose a committee to procure so much land as they shall think convenient for to set the meeting-house on, to this we dissent, for that

28

there is no land to be purchased. Our fathers in time past, whilst we belonged to Haverhill, voted and granted a piece of land for a parsonage for the west end of said town, which since by an act of incorporation of the General Court, is constituted by the name of Methuen, a township; and the aforesaid parsonage being most suitable and convenient for the inhabitants to build the meeting-house on, although in a former meeting of this town, as may be seen by the town book, and a number of freeholders and other inhabitants, did, by a pretended vote, contrary to law, or rather by a petition, carry the meeting-house to another place, which we then gave out dissent against, and do now dissent against the proceedings consequent upon said vote or petition. For a Committee to have the disposal of our estates after the manner set forth in the warrant to purchase any and is unreasonable, for that by the warrant they are invested with a power too great. Our estates ought not to lie at their will and doom. The great Charter of England lately confirmed to us by our sovereign lord, King George, wherein is contained liberty, right and property, referenced thereto being had, gives us the disposal and ordering of our estates, all debts and demands to our sovereign lord the kind being paid first. What committee then shall assess our lands by tax to pay for the purchase of land without our free consent?

4. That the said committee may procure one acre of land in some convenient place for a burying-place, to this we dissent. Our right and property that we have in voting and procuring such a place, we deny the giving of it into the hands of a committee in the manner as is expressed in the warrant. For that it is every man's right and property that belongs to the town to have his vote in the choice of a committee, or rather to vote the place where, and not to have them appointed by the Selectmen.

5. The said committee are to provide timber and to draw it to the place, or hire it drawn; we dissent; for that there is no need of making a land tax for such a thing, when every man by consent may draw his own proportion of timber, carting, &c.

6. To see whether the town will agree that every man in this town shall have an equal proportion of the common land within this town, according to what rates he shall pay in the town; we dissent first, for it is unreasonable that an hired servant, who is rated only fo rhis head, and hath no freehold, shall have an interest in our right and property; and, farther, the Providence law provides, that all persons that reside in any town for the space of twenty days, if they trade, shall be rated. By this you will give our right and land to strangers. To the particulars as above, and for the reasons annexed, we offer our dissent as freeborn

subjects to the Crown of Great Britain having an interest in the whole-some laws and liberties by and from which we expect to be protected.

In seems, however that this protest failed to convince the obstinate majority of their injustice, but work on the meeting-house went on, and the building was raised on Powder House hill. As a last resort, the minority then appealed to the "Great and General Court," in a petition that the town be ordered to set the meeting-house on Meeting-House Hill. It seems that a committee of the Legislature was then commissioned to visit Methuen to examine the important question. The only record we find of their visit is, that Richard Swan was afterwards allowed by the town one pound, ten shillings for the entertainment of the visiting states men. But, the result of it all was, that the town was ordered by the General Court to set the meeting-house on Meeting-House Hill, and accordingly, in 1727 the town voted to remove the frame to that spot, and the minority triumphed. We find from the town records that nine town-meetings were held during the first year, and that the principal business was locating the meeting-house, and perfecting the necessary arrangements for religious service. At that time, and for many years after, the minister and meeting-house were supported by a town tax, as schools and highways are now. The town records show that the Sunday Services, as well as the town-meetings were held at the house of Asie Swan until the meeting house was ready for occupancy. Asie Swan seems to have been one of the men prominent in town affairs, and his house is said to have been situated a little east of Prospect Hill. The meeting-house frame was moved in the fall of 1727, and raised on "Meeting-House Hill" on the common, a little south of the "Frye Place," where it stood for nearly seventy years. It was finished in the spring of 1728, and it appears from the town records that a town-meeting was held in the new meeting-house on Wednesday, August 28, 1728, among other purposes, "To see if the Town will order that the public worship of God should be exercised in said meeting-house," and it was voted "that the meeting for public worship should be removed from the house of Asie

Swan, and held at the meeting-house next Sabbath." It strikes one now as a little strange that a community so devout should have begun to use their house of worship without any dedicatory exercises.

The next business of the town was to get a minister. To that end, a town-meeting was called December 16, 1728, of which the first business was to "appoint a day of fasting and prayer to spread out united supplication before the Lord, for his gracious assistance and conduct in our endeavors to settle a minister amongst us, and to act such things as many be necessary in order thereunto," and Wednesday, January 2d, was appointed for that purpose. A committee was also appointed to agree with the neighboring ministers concerning keeping this fast. The records do not tell us how the fast was kept, but Robert Swan was paid twelve shillings for providing for the ministers on the day set apart for fasting and prayer.

On the third of March, 1729, it was voted "That a committee be chosen to discourse with Mr. Christopher Sargent in order to his settlement with us in the work of the ministry." Mr. Sargent, was a young man, then twenty-six years of age, a graduated a Harvard, and had been acting pastor of the congregation for some time.

It is a fact of interest showing how permanent the pastoral office was regarded in those days, that at the annual town meeting, held on March 12th, it was voted to give Mr. Sargent eighty pounds a year for the first four years, ninety pounds a year for the next four years, and after that a hundred pounds a year. Mr. Sargent's proposal was, that they should pay eighty pounds a year, and also thirty cords of wood yearly from the time he began to keep house. After considerable discussion between Mr. Sargent and the people, the terms of settlement were agreed upon, and he was ordained pastor over the church November 5, 1729. Of the festivities, which attended that occasion we have no record, but there is no doubt that the day was celebrated according to the customs of the time, with great rejoicing, and by all the people round about.

The new town now seems to have fairly started on its career, and little is to be found in the records worthy of notice. The town meetings were frequent, and the business transacted in those meetings in the different years much the same. The officers of the town were chosen then, as now, in the month of March.

The officers were about the same as now, with the addition of tithing men and the exception of School Committee.

Persons were annually chosen "to clear the fishways" and "to take care that the fish have a convenient course over Mr. Huse's Mill Dam that is in Spicket River."

Two persons called deer reeves were also chosen annually for many years to take care of the deer, and a reward was generally offered, each year for the killing of a grown wolf, a smaller one for "a bitch wolf's whelp."

Each bill against the town, however small, seems to have been presented to the town meeting for allowance; and there was, nearly every year, one or more for roads laid out by the selectmen and accepted by the town.

The amount of money annually appropriated for town charges, outside of the minister rate, for the first fifty years, ranged from forty to one hundred and seventy pounds. This does not include the highway tax, which was paid in labor, and of which we find record in 1736.

In 1735, Henry Saunders and twenty-eight others living in the north part of the town,–probably most of them in what is now Salem, N.H., presented a petition to the town setting forth that:

> Whereas we, the subscribers, live at so great a distance from the public worship of God in this place, that we cannot attend upon it with our families without a great deal of difficulty, we have therefore been at the charge to hire a minister to preach to us in a more convenient place,

which we think is hard for us to do, so long as we are obliged to pay our full proportion towards the support of the public worship of God in this place; and although we have of late made out application to this town for some help under our difficult circumstances, we have been denied any. We therefore pray that you would set us off a distinct precinct by ourselves.

This petition was presented to the town December 15, 1735, and the record says:

That the town, by a majority vote, manifested their willingness to set off the north part of town for a precinct by themselves, viz.; Beginning at the north side of the World's End Pond, so running easterly to the south side of Peter Merrill's land, and so to Haverhill line, and from World's End Pond, to a wading place in Spicket River by Jonathan Corliss', and so running with a straight line to a pine tree standing in the line between Dracut and Methuen, on the south side of Porcupine Brook.

The territory north of this line formed what was afterwards known as the North Parish of Methuen, and most of it soon after fell within the limits of New Hampshire.

The relative number of inhabitants in the two parishes at that time cannot be exactly determined.

The nearest approach to a correct estimate may perhaps be made from the statement that the number of highway tax payers in 1736, in the whole town, was one hundred and thirty-six. The number of tax payers of the minister rate in the First Parish in that year was ninety-eight, leaving thirty-eight in the North-Parish.

The next important event in the history of the town occurred in 1741, when the State line was run, thereby depriving Methuen of a large part of her territory. Previous to 1740, there seems to have been much controversy between the Province of Massachusetts and New Hampshire about the boundary line between them. The charter first given to the Massachusetts colony granted "all that part of New England lying between three miles to the north of the Merrimack and three miles to the south of the Charles River, and of every part thereof in the Massachusetts Bay; and in length between the described breadth from the Atlantic Ocean to the South Sea." Under the charter, the Massachusetts colony claimed that their boundary was three miles to the north of the northernmost point of the Merrimack, and they fixed upon a rock near the outlet of Lake Winnipisseogee, as he most northern part of the river. This would have given to Massachusetts a large part of Vermont and New Hampshire, and a large section in Maine. The New Hampshire grantees claimed that under the Massachusetts charter the line could not extend in any place more than three miles from the river. The territory between these lines became disputed ground concerning which there was constant contention.

In 1720 the New Hampshire colonists modified their claim, so far as to propose that the line should begin at a point three miles north from the mouth of the Merrimack, and thence run due west to the South Sea. The Massachusetts colony refused to agree to this and the contention become more violent, until the Legislatures of the two colonies met–the New Hampshire Legislature at Hampton Falls and the Massachusetts at Salisbury—for the purpose of settling the difficulty. They appointed committees of conference, but were unable to agree, and after several weeks of angry discussion by agreement of both parties the whole subject was referred to the King of England for decision. The matter was decided by the king in council in 1740, and it was decreed that the northern boundary of the Province of Massachusetts Bay, "is and be a similar curved line, pursuing the curve of Merrimack River at three miles distance, on the north side thereof and beginning at the Atlantic Ocean." The king also decreed that the line should be run and established by the two Provinces, but if either should refuse to act, the other might fix and establish it.

Massachusetts was dissatisfied with this decision, and refused to have anything to do about running the new line. New Hampshire appointed George Mitchell to run the line from the ocean to a point three miles north of Pawtucket Falls, and the line was thus established by New Hampshire as it has been recognized by the border towns on both sides of the line ever since. Massachusetts has never formally agreed to this line, and the old controversy has been recently revived. Commissioners were appointed by both States in 1885 to settle this question, if possible, and they have not yet completed their work. Tradition says that this decision was brought about by sharp practice on the part of the agent appointed by New Hampshire to lay the subject before the king; and it gave to New Hampshire seven hundred square miles more than she asked for. It cut off a large slice of the original territory of the town of Methuen, and nearly a third of the population. The northern and western boundaries of the town have remained unchanged from that time to the present. From 1740 to 1775, we find record of very few important events.

COLONIAL PERIOD.

There was no census until 1765 but we judge from the increase in the number of taxpayers, that the growth was simply the slow and steady increase of an exclusively agricultural population. As the land gradually became cleared, it became more thickly dotted with dwellings. The produce raised upon the farms, and food taken from the river supplied nearly all the wants of the inhabitants. The money necessary for their few purchases, and the payment of taxes, was obtained partly by the sale of wood and timber which was rafted to Newburyport, partly by the production of flax which was sold to the inhabitants of London-derry, and partly, probably, by the sale of some products, such as they would carry on horseback to Salem. We find little information on the part Methuen had in the French and Indian Wars. Two or three extra appropriations for powder and flints, some taxes abated to those who were in the service, and payments of money by the town for "taking care of the French" seem to be all that shows action on the part of the town. Tradition has it that Methuen sent her share of soldiers at that time, but whether there was a company from the town, or whether the soldiers were scattered among different companies from neighboring towns we have no means of knowing.

There seems to have been at this time a remarkable reluctance to hold office, as is shown by the fact that Methuen was fined in 1770, '72, and '73, for not choosing a Representative to the Legislature. Possibly, however, this may have resulted more from a disinclination on the part of the taxpayers to pay for the service, than from a disinclination to serve on the part of the possible candidates. In 1774, the inhabitants of the west part of Methuen petitioned to be set off with the easterly part of Dracut to make a new township, "so that both the above said towns may be better accommodated to attend public worship." The division line of the proposed new town, commenced "on the bank of the Merrimack River about four poles to the east of Mr. Daniel Bodwell's ferry (at the foot of Tower Hill); thence running northwesterly to the province line, about one hundred and fifty-six poles to the west of Spicket River, including all to the west of said line." this cutting off a large portion of the town. There was a strong opposition on the part of Methuen, and the scheme failed. About this time, we begin to find indications of the coming contest. The first record we find of any action by the town in relation to the questions then stirring the public mind, is a vote passed in August 1774, to pay one pound, sixteen shillings and seven pence, lawful money to defray the charges of the Congress held at Philadelphia. In December, 1774, it was voted that Mr. Enoch Merrill, former constable should pay the remainder of the province money to Henry Gardner, and also "that the Selectmen should conduct themselves respecting the Constable's warrants according to the Provincial Congress instructions." A that time the constables collected the taxes, and paid them over under instructions of the selectmen, and the meaning of these votes probably was, that the province tax was to be paid under the instructions of the Provincial Congress rather than the English Government.

METHUEN IN THE REVOLUTION.

No other record of action at that time appears in the regular records of the town, but on one of the last leaves of the book of records then in use, we find the following:

at a leggel meeting of the freeholders and other inhabitants of the Town of Methuen held by adjournment from the ninth of August, 1774, to the 20th of September, 1774. Taking into serious consideration the State of public affairs, Voted, that a Committee be chosen to consult and Advise with Each other. Likewise with Committees of other Towns, and if need be to communicate to any other Town any measure that we may appear to be conducive to the publick Benefite, more Especlay to be Watch-full that no Encroachments are not made on our Constitutional Rights and Liberties, that we may enjoy the Blessing we have Left in peace and not be Deprived of them from any quarter but may Devise prosecute the most vigorous and resolute measures as far as Lyes in our sphere, retrieved our invaluable privileges. Voted that this Committee consist of fifteen persons.

	James Jones
Stephen Barker, Esq.	John Huse
John Bodwell	James Malloon
Nathaniel Pettengill	John Pettengill
Samuel Bodwell	Lieut. John Sargent
Cutting Marsh	Richard Whittier
David Whittier	Ebenezer Colten
Jonathan Swan	John Masten

Voted, that they above should be entered in the Town Clerk's office.

That the people began to contemplate the war with Great Britain is indicated by the following, which is an exact copy of the original now in possession of A.C. Goodell, Esq., of Salem. Ma.

Whereas, military Exercise hath been much nelicked We the subscribers being the first comptrey in Methuen Do Covenant and Engage to form our savels in to a Bodey in order to Larn the manual Exercise, to be Subegat To Such officers as the Comptrey shall chuse by Voat in all constutenal marsher according to our Chattaers.[sic]

"Methuen ye 6th of Octr.1774
James Jones

Ichabod Perkins	Jacob Hall
James Wilson	Amos Gage
Timothy Eaton	John Cross
Ebenezer Calton	Nathan Russ
Thomas Runnels	Richard Jaques
Henry Morss	Robert Hastings
Samuel Messer	James Chase
Daniel Messer	Nath. Herrick
Nath'l Haseltine	Joseph Hastings
Richard Hall	Kimball Carlton
Samuel Parker	Richard Currier
William Runnels	Ebenezer Eaton
Asa Currier	Simeon Hastens
Nathaniel Messer	John Howe, Jr.
Ebenzer Messer	Farnum Hall
Nathan Perley	Ephraim Clark
John Keley	John Marsen, Jr.
Asa Messer	Nathaniel Smith Messer
John Eaton	James Silver, Jnr
John Davison	Abiel How
William Stevens	Timothy Emerson
Silas Brown	Joshua Emerson, Jr.
William Whittier	Oliver Emerson
Stephen Webster, Jr.	Timothy How
Jacob Messer	Isaac Barker
Daniel R. Whittier	Simeon Cross
Samuel Webber	Francis Swan, Junr.

James Davison	Asa Morss
Jacob How	Nath'l Clark
Elijah Carlton	John Merrill
Joseph How	Abiel Cross
Jonathan How	Theodore Emerson

The first Compyney in Methuen meat att Mr. Eben Carlton's in order to chuse officers, and thay chose Lieut. Benj'm Hall Moderator. They chose Mr. James Jones for that Capt. Mr. Ichobied Perkins furst Leut. Mr. James Wilson second Leut. Mr. Sam'l Messer Ens. Mr. Nath'l Messer Jr. Clark for said Compyney.

William Page Clark for sd. Metten.

Methuen ye 6 of October 1774.

In January 1775, the town voted to give to the poor of the town of Boston by subscription, and chose a committee to receive donations. At the same meeting it was voted that the minute-men "drawn out of exposed to train, should have eight pence per day for their trouble to the last of March."

Mr. John Bodwell was also chosen at that meeting to meet the Provincial Congress on the first day of February at Cambridge. At the annual meeting in March it was voted to provide bayonets, "which should be brought to Captain John Davis, and after the service as over said Davis is to return said bayonets unto the selectmen of said town." It was also voted that the committee for the same purpose, and also that John Masters and Jonathan Barker be a committee to make up the "cartrages" for those persons who were not able to provide for themselves, out of the town stock. Soon after, the town voted to provide guns for all minute men unable to furnish themselves; also to provide blankets and cartridges.

Another interesting document, dated about this time, is also found out of place on one of the last leaves of the book of records, as follows:—

We, the subscribers, being appointed a committee by the town of Methuen to give some instructions to a certain Committee of Safety and Correspondence that was chosen by this town in September last

39

or may hereafter be chosen as above, that it is recommended that the above committee do strictly observe and conform to the instructions hereafter mentioned.

First. That you will be vigilant in this time of public distress; that no infractions, violations be made in the good and wholesome laws of this province, whereby the morals of the people are endangered of being corrupted, and in case you should be unsuccessful in your endeavors in all proper ways, then to publish their names that the public may see and known them to be enemies of their country and the privileges of the same.

Secondly. That you correspond with committees of other towns, if you see it needful, as may be necessary on all important occasions.

Thirdly. As a Committee of Inspection we recommend to you that you will not buy or purchase any British manufactures or superfluities in your families but such as are of absolute necessity, and likewise that you recommend to others to do the same, for we think that a reformation of this will greatly tend to lessen out private expense and the better enable us to bear the publick charges and prevent those mischiefs that may ensue thereupon.

Fourthly. That you will suppress as much as possible those persons, if any such there be, who travel as peddlers to introduce British goods and impose on the inconsiderate, which may impoverish us. And whereas, it is said that our enemies are sending out spies in order to get information of our schemes and plans which are contrived for our defense so as they may frustrate them, it is recommended that you take care that they received that resentment due to their deeds.

Fifthly. If any trader or other person within this town shall take the advantage of the present distressed circumstances in America and by an avaricious thirst after gain shall raise the price of any commodity whatsoever beyond their usual reasonable price, or shall use their influence by words of actions to weaken the measures advise be they Grand Continental Congress when made to appear to you that he or they persist in the same, you are to publish their names that they may be publickly known and treated as enemies to their country.

James Ingalls   Committee
Jonathan Swan   Methuen April 4th, 1775
John Huse

40

It will be noticed that this paper was dated about two weeks before the battle of Lexington. It shows the resolute, deep-seated earnestness with which our fathers entered the contest, and that the men of Methuen were as fully imbued with the spirit of resistance to tyranny as the more widely known men of the time. As might be expected, the town records are silent in regard to the events as Lexington and Bunker Hill. There was no reason why the town as a body should take action in reference to those battles. Nevertheless, the men of Methuen had an active share in those great events, and we are not without an official record of the part they took.

The archives at the State House contain the names of those who went from Methuen on the memorable 19th of April, and also the names of the Methuen Company who fought at the battle of Bunker Hill.

There were four Methuen companies at the battle of Lexington, and the following is a full list of the names just as they are found on the original muster rolls now on file in the office of the Secretary of State:

Captain John Davis Company in Colonel Frye's Regiment, enlisted Feb 14th 1775.

Captain, John Davis,

First Lieutenant, Nathl. Herrick,

Second Lieutenant Eliphalet Bodwell,

Sergeants. Eleazar Carleton, Francis Swan, Richard Hall, Jona. Barker,

Corporals. Jonathan Baxter, John Davison, William Stevens, Joshua Emerson,

Privates

James Campbell,	Simeon Tyler,
Silas Brown,	Amos Harriman,
Enos Kings,	Daniel Jennings,
Asa Morse,	Wm. Whitcher,
Ebenr. Pingrief,	Nathan Swan,

Peter Barker,
Joseph Jackson,
Aaron Noyes,
Parker Bodwell,
Daniel Morse,
James Ordway,
Ebenezer Herrick,
Daniel Messer,
Nathan Russ,
James Ingalls,
James Davison,
Amos Gage (Drummer),
Joseph Morse,
Dudley Noyes,

Joseph Hibbard,
Prince Johnnot,
Solomon Jennings,
Joshua Bodwell,
Dudley Bailey,
James Silver,
Peter Webster,
John Swan,
Daniel Bailey,
Thomas Bace,
Jeremiah Stevens,
Ebenezer Sargent,
John Merrill,
Samuel Barker (fifer),

This muster roll made for seven days, from April 19th. Sworn to John Davis.

Total , 49.

Muster roll of the following number of party of men that belonged to Methuen, in the country of Essex, on the alarm on the 19th of April, 1775, a never joined to any particular commanding officer:

Captain James Mallon.

Privates.

Abner Morrill,
Isaac Austin,
Isaac Austin, Jr.,
Benj. Herrick,
Peter Harris,
Joseph Griffin,
Francis Richardson,
Elisha Parker,
John Parker, Jr.,
Isaac Hughs,
Timothy Chellis,
—Bodwell, 2d. ,

—Austin, Jr. ,
—Parker, Jr.,
Obadiah Morse,
W'm. Russ, Jr.
Wm. McCleary,
Hezekiah Parker,
Jesse Barker,
Moses Morse,
James Dennis,

Total, 22.

The pay roll of the company under the command of Major Samuel Bodwell, exhibited in consequence of the alarm on the 19th of April:

1st Lieut., David Whittier,

Ensign, Enoch Merrill,

2nd Lieut. Nathl. Pettengill,

Clerk, John Hughs,

Sergeant, John Mansur

Privates

Wm. Gutterson,
Nath'l Pettengill,
Thomas Pettengill,
Dudley Pettengill,
Daniel Tyler,
John Pettengill, Jr.,
Sam'l Cross,
John Bodwell,
Parker Richardson,
Thos. Dow,
Wm. Bodwell,
Wm. Morse,
John Barker,
Simeon Dow,
Samuel Cole,
Samuel Hughs,
John Pettengill,
John Webber,
Benj. Mastin,
Elijah Sargent,
Joshua Stevens,

John Whittier, Jr.,
Abel Merrill,
Joseph Merrill,
John Richardson,
Wm. Richardson,
Nath'l Hibbard,
James Hibbard,
Bodwell Ladd,
John Ladd,
Stephen Barker,
Mitchell Davis,
Eben'r Barker,
Nehemiah Barker,
Sam'l Richardson,
Enoch Cheney,
Jona. Barker, Jr.,
Benj. Stevens, J.,
John Hibbard, Jr.,
Wm. Hibbard.

Total 45

Capt. James Jones pay roll for the campaign on the defence of the country at the battle at Concord, made at the rate of twenty-eight days per month, four days service:

Captain, James Jones,

Lieutenant, Ichabod Perkins

Sergeants, Timothy Eaton, Ephraim Clark, Nathan Perley, Jacob
    Messer

Corporals. Nath'l Haseltine, Elijah Carleton, Simeon Cross,

Privates

John Kelly (Drummer),
John Tippets, 3d.,
Abiel Cross,
Oliver Emerson,
William Page,
James Messer,
Moses Sargent,
Henry Mors,
James Fry,
Stephen Webster, Jr.,
Thomas Herrick,
Elisha Perkins,

Joseph Granger,
Job Pingrey,
Isaac Barker,
Joseph Cross,
Day Emerson,
Joseph Perkins,
John Morris,
Jona. How,
Kimball Carleton,
Nath'l S. Clark,

Total 32

In the Company of Capt. Charles Furbush:.

Privates

Theodore Emerson,
James Silver,
Isaac Maloon,
John Hancock,
Jos. Pettengill,
Nehemiah Kidah,
Abraham P. Silver,
Daniel Pettengill.
    Total 8

Grand Total 156.

The number of inhabitants in Methuen in 1776, according to the Colonial Census, was thirteen hundred and twenty-six.

The tax book of that year gives the names of two hundred and fifty-two poll tax payers.

44

It is surprising that a town of so small population could have sent so many men at the first call to meet the British. Nothing could more forcibly impress us with the universal, deep-seated determination of our fathers to protect their rights at all hazards, than this simple list of names. When we consider that they were not called out by any other of the authorities, that their enthusiasm had not been stirred by appeals from the daily press or by public speakers, that they only knew from the signal guns and fires on the hills that the British were in motion, and that the war had actually begun, and that nearly every able bodied man in town, more than half the poll-tax payers, must, of their own accord, have shouldered their muskets and marched at a moment's warning to meet the foe, those of us who claim descent from those men cannot help feeling the blood tingle in our veins with an honest pride in such an ancestry. Such facts show better than anything else can, the quality of the Revolutionary spirit, and how it was that the colonies were finally successful. The next important event was the battle of Bunker Hill on the 17th of June following, in which it is certain that a Methuen company bore an important part. The following is a copy of the original muster roll on the file at the State House.

Cambridge, Oct. 5, 1775.

Return of the men s names, when they enlisted, and where they belonged. Belonging to Capt. John Davis Company in Col. Frye s Regiment:

Captain, John Davis,

1st Lieutenant Nath'l Herrick,

2nd Lieutenant Eliphalet Bodwell,

Major, Jonathan Barker,

Sergeants, Ebenezer Carleton, Francis Swan, Richard Hall, Peter Barker

Corporals, Jonathan Baxter, Joshua Emerson, William Stevens, John Davison,

Abraham Anness,	Samuel Parker,
Lazarus Hubbard,	James Silver,
John Asten,	Thomas Pace,
Ebenezer Herrick (died June 17th),	Simeon Tyler,
Silas Brown,	Nathan Russ,
Joseph Hibbard (died June 20th),	Amos Gage (Drummer),
Parker Bodwell,	John Swan,
James Ingalls (died July 8th),	Samuel Barker (Fifer),
David Bailey,	Nathan Swan,
Aaron Noyes,	James Campbell,
Timothy Chellis,	Ebenezer Pingrief,
Peter Webster,	James Davison,
David Corliss,	Joshua Bodwell (in train July
James Woodbury,	17th),
James Ordway,	Michel Davis,
Ebenezer Sargent,	Solomon Jennings (in train
Jeremiah Stevens,	July 17th),
	Amos Harriman,

It is by no means certain that this list includes the names of all Methuen men engaged in the battle; there may have been some in companies from the neighboring towns. It is known that the Methuen Company was in the thickest of the fight that it was stationed in the redoubt, and was among the last to leave it. It is said that it came near being surround towards the end of the battle, and that as the enemy came up on each hand a British soldier ran up to Captain Davis, saying, "You are my prisoner."

Captain Davis, who was a resolute, powerful man, replied, "I guess not," at the same time running the soldier through with his sword. The blood spurted over his breeches as he drew back the sword, but he made his escape. It is also said that Captain Davis took one of his wounded men upon his back just after escaping from the redoubt, and carried him out of the reach of danger. As he was crossing the hollow between the hills, which were swept by the fire from a British vessel, he saw before him a board fence. Captain Davis, tired by excitement and the weight of this comrade, said: "I don't see how we can get over that fence." But an instant after, a cannon ball knocked it in pieces and left the way clear.

Mr. Asa M. Bodwell tells a story of James Ordway, who afterwards lived on the west side of Tower Hill. Mr. Ordway was in poor circumstances in his old age, and had a bad ulcer on his leg. Mr. Bodwell says that his father sent him one day to Mr. Ordway with a gallon of rum to bathe him lame leg, and with it a message saying that the rum was sent to pay for throwing stones at the battle of Bunker Hill. The story being, that when the ammunition gave out, at the close of the battle, Ordway laid down his gun and threw stones at the British until driven out. Methuen lost three men at the battle of Bunker Hill. Ebenezer Herrick was killed in the battle, Joseph Hibbard was wounded and died June 20th, James Ingalls was wounded and died July 8th. It is impossible to ascertain the exact number of soldiers Methuen had in the Revolutionary War. The town records give us no information on this point, and the State records are imperfect, but there is no doubt that Methuen kept her quota in the field. After the evacuation of Boston by the British, the seat of war was so far away, that probably few of the soldiers from this town were actively engaged with the enemy.

There are stories told of Methuen men who went to fight Burgoyne, and helped to conduct the captured soldiers to Cambridge, and guard them while there; other soldiers from this town were stationed at different points on the coast exposed to attack.

During those years, the town business went on as usual. A Committee of Safety and Correspondence was appointed each year, and in February 1778, the town voted that the Selectmen should supply the families of soldiers in the Continental Army with the necessaries of life. At the same meeting the town was called upon to see what instructions it would give to their Representative, relative to a resolve of the Continental Congress for all the United States of America to join in a perpetual union with one another. The subject was referred to a committee, consisting of Major Bodwell, Captain James Jones, Colonel Thomas Poor, Lieutenant John Huse and Mr. Enoch Merrill. At an adjourned meeting, the question was put whether the town would receive and accept the Articles of Confederation and perpetual union, and "voted in the affirmative."

The currency question seems to have been as troublesome in those days as it as been later. At a meeting held April 2, 1778, there was an article in the warrant "To see what the town will do with those persons who refuse to take our paper currency,—and passed a resolve to treat them as enemies to their country, and voted to publish the same in the Boston newspaper." The rapid decrease in value of this currency is shown by the fact, that while, in 1777, £30 was raised for the ordinary repairs of the high-ways, in 1781 £6000 was raised for the same purpose.

In 1779, Lieut. John Sargent was chosen delegate to represent the town in the convention to be held in Cambridge, to form a new constitution. In 1780, the new Constitution of the State of Massachusetts took effect, and in that year we find the first record of a vote for Governor and Senators. It is evident that party feeling did not run very high, from the fact that for the office of Governor, John Hancock had sixty-four votes and James Bowdoin two.

In that year, the town furnished 8780 pounds of beef for the army, and hired sixteen men. The next year furnished 6057 pounds of beef, and raised twelve men to serve as soldiers.

We find nothing in the town records to indicate the end of the war, except a vote to sell the entrenching tools belonging to the town, and the frequency of military titles, indicating that the soldiers were at home, and active in town matters.

FERRYS, BRIDGES AND TURNPIKES.

From the close of the Revolutionary War, there is little of interest to be gleaned from the town records for many years. About this time, we find that the town voted "not to give liberty for inoculation for small-pox," and to "choose a committee of five to take care of those persons lately inoculated with the small-pox, and prosecute them, and take effectual care that the distemper spread no further."

In 1793, a company was organized to build a bridge over the Merrimack at Bodwell's Falls. Up to that time, ferries had furnished the only means of crossing this river. We find mention of five different ferries, as follows:

Gage's Ferry, near the end of Pleasant Valley Street.
Swan's Ferry, at Wingate Farm.
Marston's Ferry, at the Alms-house, Lawrence
Bodwell's Ferry, at the Pumping Station, Lawrence
Harris's Ferry, a little east of the Dracut line.

The early inhabitants did not dream that a bridge could be built across so broad a stream, and a common way of expressing the impossibility of doing a thing was to say, "It is impossible as to build a bridge over the Merrimack River." It seems, too, that some of the inhabitants did not take kindly to the new project, probably deeming it a base scheme on the part of the proprietors to make money out of the public; for a meeting was held soon after to see if the town would send a remonstrance to the General Court against its erection. This proposition was decided in the negative. The opponents of the bridge then called a meeting to see if the town would petition the General Court to order the proprietors to pay the cost of the town roads leading to the bridge. This also was voted down, and the town decided to repair the road over Currant's Hill to the New Hampshire line.

The bridge was built shortly after, and for some years the travel from thence to New Hampshire passed over Currant's Hill, curving around over the old road–now discontinued–on the hill in the rear of the house of James Ingalls.

The "Turnpike" (now Broadway) was built in 1805-6, by an incorporated company. A system of toll was established, but it caused such dissatisfaction that in a few years the "Turnpike" was made a public highway by the County Commissioners.

POST-COLONIAL METHUEN.

The town first voted for a Representative to Congress and for a Presidential Elector, December 18, 1788, the highest candidate voted for receiving twenty-three votes. It seems that at the first Presidential elections, the town voted for only one elector; but in 1804 votes were case for nineteen electors.

The change from the use of English money to Federal currency took place about 1795-96. The last time we find "pounds" used in making up the town records was in 1795.

In 1805, the town voted that the Annual Town Meeting should be held on the first Monday, in March, for the future; and, at the same meeting, for the first time voted that that swine should not go at large. Previous to that time, the town had always voted the largest liberty to swine, except that for a few years this liberty had been coupled with the condition that they should be "yoaked and ringed."

In the War of 1812, Methuen sent her proportion of men to meet the old enemy. The only reference to that war in the town records is a vote passed "to give the detached soldiers a sum to make them up twelve dollars a month while in active service with what Government gives them." We have been told by veterans of that war, now dead, that the number of men called for from Methuen was not large. They were mostly stationed to defend the forts along the coast. It is said, however, that a small number of soldiers went from Methuen to meet the British in Canada, and that they were present at the surrender to Hull. It appears from the census returns and the tax lists that Methuen grew but little in wealth and population, during the forty years subsequent to the Revolutionary War. In 1776 the population of the town numbered one thousand three hundred and twenty-six, and in 1820 one thousand three hundred and seventy one.

There was no village in the town at that time, and no neighboring markets to induce growth. At the beginning of this century there were only six houses in the now thickly settled part of Methuen Village. The Miller Cross house, corner of Hampshire and Lowell Streets,; Sargent house, where Exchange Hotel stands; Deacon Fry house, Butters farm; Swan place, Nevins farm; Jonathan Cluff house, Mill-yard; John Sargent house, at elm tree by mill-yard.

There was then one grist-mill, a little south of Fisher's grocery store, another on the opposite side of the river, and a fulling-mill just below the foot-bridge at the falls. From 1820-1840 the town gained about seventy per cent, in population, with a corresponding increase in wealth. This was in consequence of the building of the cotton mills, and increase in the manufacture of shoes and hats.

During that time there were few events of special interest to this generation. In 1837, in appears that a new town-house was talked about, and a committee was chosen at the March meeting to select a location and prepare estimates. The committee reported at a adjourned meeting, and the town voted to build. A week or two afterwards another meeting was called, the vote reconsidered and committee discharge. The same year the selectmen were authorized to hire the vestry of the Baptist meeting-house for holding town-meetings and that house continued to be the place for town-meetings until the present town-house was built in 1853. In 1844, rumors began to circulate of a project a dam the Merrimack, and build factories at Bodwell's Falls. The town voted to give Daniel Saunders and his associates a refusal of the town farm, which was situated on Broadway, the buildings being on the east side, south of Haverhill Street, at its cost, with an addition of thirty-three per cent.

The terms on which the Essex Company bonded the land now occupied by the principal parts of the city of Lawrence were a fair cash value, with an addition of thirty-three per cent. The land was bough in due time, and the "New City" as it was then called, grew with wonderful rapidity. When operations first began there were only nine or ten houses standing on what is now the thickly settled part of North Lawrence. There was a paper-mill, operated by Adolphus Durant, on the Spicket a little above its mouth. In 1847, Chas. S. Storrow and others petitioned for an act of incorporation or a new town to be called Lawrence. There was a strong opposition to this scheme on the part of Methuen, a town-meeting was called, and John Tenney and George A. Waldo were chosen to oppose the petition before the committee of the Legislature. They were unsuccessful in this opposition; Lawrence obtained an act of incorporation, and Methuen lost a large section of her territory. Another small slice was subsequently taken from Methuen and added to Lawrence, since which time the boundaries of Methuen have remained unchanged.

CIVIL WAR.

Doubtless of old residents of the town will recall many matters of much interest in their day, such as bickerings about the enforcement of the liquor laws, the efforts made to suppress the liquor traffic in Salem, the contests over the building of new roads, but they would hardly be of general interest now. From 1850-1860 there was little change in population and few events of general interest. In 1861, came the war, which laid its hand so heavily on the whole land. When the first note of war was sounded, and President Lincoln called for seventy-five thousand troops to protect Washington in April 1861, Governor Andrew ordered the Sixth Massachusetts Regiment, with others, to start at once. Company F of that Regiment, Capt. Charbourne, had its armory in Lawrence and eight members of that company belonged in Methuen as follows:

Henry Cummings,
Albert L. Dame,
Amos G. Jones,
George Keny,
Frank Sanborn,
George Thurlow,
James Troy,
Henry Tarkington,

They were notified of the call late in the afternoon, and immediately reported for duty, and the next morning they all left Lawrence for Washington. On the 19th, they made the memorable passage through Baltimore where they met the first resistance to the Federal troops. This Methuen has had the honor of seeing her sons foremost in the fight in both of our great wars; for as Lexington and Concord were the initial events in the Revolutionary War, so was Baltimore in the Civil War.

The first action taken by the town was immediately afterwards on April 30th, when a town-meeting was held, and the sum of five thousand dollars voted the purpose of arming, equipping and furnishing volunteers. A committee consisting of the selectmen, Eben. Sawyer, J.P. Flint, John C. Webster and Daniel Currier was appointed to disbursed the money." A company was at once formed, all of the volunteers from Methuen and vicinity, and most of them from Methuen and they were uniformed, equipped and drilled, so as to be ready for action. This company became Company B, Fourteenth Massachusetts Infantry, and for some time, was stationed at Fort Warren, and

53

went to Washington in the latter part of the summer of 1861. In August of that year, the town voted to pay State aid to the families of volunteers according to the law.

In July 1862, forty-seven men were called for, and the town voted to pay a bounty of one hundred dollars to each volunteer when mustered into the United States service. On the 2nd of August, the town held another meeting, in which it as voted to pay two hundred dollars in addition to the sum already voted, making three hundred in all, to volunteers when mustered into the service. Immediately after came another from the President for three hundred thousand nine month's men. A meeting was at once called to adopt measures to obtain the number required from Methuen. It was voted to pay one hundred and fifty dollars to each nine-month's man when mustered in and credited to the town.

The next call for recruits came in November 1863, and the town voted "to fill its quota under the call for three hundred thousand men." A vote also passed to pay the families of drafted men the same State aid that was paid to families of volunteers.

In May 1866, the selectmen were authorized to pay one hundred and twenty-five dollars bounty to volunteers in anticipation of a call from the President for more men. After this time, however, few recruits were mustered in. The volunteers from Methuen were scattered through several different regiments, but the largest number was in Company B, First Massachusetts Heavy Artillery, which was noted as a remarkably well-drilled and disciplined body of men. When the regiments were detailed for the defense of Washington, the Fourteenth Massachusetts Infantry was selected after a competitive inspection with other regiments, for their excellent discipline, well-regulated camp, good appearance, and reliable men.

The name of the regiment was changed from the Fourteenth Massachusetts Infantry to the First Massachusetts Heavy Artillery, and then men remained on duty in the forts in front of

Washington, on Arlington Heights, until towards the end of the war, when they were ordered to the front, and performed distinguished service. They were engaged in sixteen to twenty different battles, and at Spotsylvania they occupied an important position in the center of Grant's army, and held at bay Ewell's force of more than four times their number, until reinforcements arrived from a distance of five miles, thus preventing Grant's army from being cut in two. For their heroic behavior on that occasion they received the unusual distinction of a special commendation from General Grant. The Methuen men received their heaviest blow in this battle, where fifteen were killed and many more wounded. The news that the company from Methuen had suffered heavily in this battle caused great excitement throughout the town, and it meeting of the citizens was immediately held. Resolutions expressive of sympathy and condolence were passed and it was voted to send an agent to look after the wounded.

It ought to be mentioned also that the Methuen Company held an honorable position in this regiment of eighteen hundred men. At the battle of June 16, the regimental color-bearer was twice shot down. Our well-known townsman, Albert L. Dame, was then given this honorable and dangerous place in the regiment, and had the honor of carrying the colors to the end of the war, and delivering them up to the State. The number of men lost from Methuen during the war was fifty-two, exclusive of those serving in the navy. According to General Schouler, the town furnished three hundred and twenty-five men for the war, which was a surplus of fifty-one over and above all demands. Fifteen were commissioned officers. The whole amount of money appropriated and expended by the town, on account of the war, exclusive of State aid, was $38,651.73.

In addition to this amount, seven thousand five hundred dollars were gratuitously given by individual citizens to aid soldiers' families and to encourage recruiting. The total amount of State aid, which has been paid to soldiers and their families in Methuen up to January 1, 1887 is $56,747.03. There were about a thousand dollars in money raised by fairs and levees, and the ladies of Methuen devoted a great deal of time to work for the soldiers.

There were two societies, the Sanitary Commission and Christian Commission, which performed a vast amount of work, whose value cannot be measured in dollars and cents. Thus it appears that there must have been paid out in Methuen, directly on account of the war, considerably more than $100,000.

As we look back over the record of Methuen in the Civil War, on the readiness with which her men mustered in the field, and the heartiness with which they were supported by those left at home, we cannot deny that this generation has proved itself worthy its Revolutionary ancestry.

SESQUICENTENNIAL.

On the 7th of September, 1876, Methuen celebrated the one hundred and fiftieth anniversary of its incorporation of the town. The day was fine and the event was observed with great enthusiasm. The booming of cannon in the early morning aroused the slumberers in the valley of the Spicket, and gave the signal for the festivities of the day to begin.

The Town-House and most private dwellings were tastefully decorated, business was suspended and the busy town took on a holiday appearance quite unusual. The exercises of the day began with a procession, composed of a cavalcade of horsemen, a military company improvised for the occasion, part equipped in the old style and part of the new, the fire department, carriages representing the different trades and business of the town, school children, distinguished visitors and citizens in carriages, making quite an imposing display. Governor Rice, Surgeon Gen. Dale, Allen W. Dodge and Hon. Carroll D. Wright, were among the visitors. The president of the day was

Hon. Jacob Emerson, orator, Hon. John H. Tarbox, chief marshal, adjutant James Ingalls, chaplain, Rev. Lyman H. Blake.

The procession, with bands of music, passed through the principal streets of the town to the "Barker Lot," near the corner of Lowell and Barker Streets, where a stand had been erected. Here an eloquent oration was delivered before a large audience, by Hon. John K. Tarbox, a son of Methuen. After the oration a banquet was served under a large tent nearby, at the conclusion of which speeches were made by the orator of the day, Hon. Allen W. Dodge, a treasurer of Essex County, Rev. Dr. A. A. Miner once pastor of a church in Methuen, Hon. Carroll D. Wright, Hon. J. C. Blaisdell of Fall River, Hon, J. K. Jenners, mayor of Haverhill, Major George S. Merrill, of Lawrence, Rev. Moses How of New Bedford and several others.

Rev. Moses How was a resident of Methuen in his youthful days, and at this time, though eight-seven years of age, a hale and vigorous man. After giving his audience many interesting reminiscences of old Methuen, he stated that he had preached eight thousand sermons, attended two thousand two hundred and sixty-five funeral, married one thousand nine hundred and four couples and had distributed five thousand two hundred and eleven Bibles and fifteen thousand Testaments to seamen. The day closed with social and family reunions at the homes of citizens of the town.

The occasion will be long remembered by those who participated in it, for the good fellowship which characterized the day, and the greetings of the sons and daughters of the town, who had come back to revisit the old homestead, revive the memories of early days and take once more by the hand the companions of their youth.

From the close of the Civil War to the present time, the town has passed through the most prosperous period of its history. The population has increased from two-thousand five hundred and seven in 1865, to four thousand five hundred and seven in 1885, and the wealth of the town has gained in like proportion.

The territorial limits have not been changed, although there has been a desire on the part of some to annex Methuen to Lawrence, The gain has been almost entirely in the thickly settled portions and has been due partly to proximity to Lawrence, but principally to an increase in manufacturing enterprises.

SCHOOLS.

The founders of Methuen seem to have provided for the educational interests of the town at an early date. In 1729 it was voted to lay out a school lot and a parsonage lot north of World's End Pond. These were undoubtedly tracts of woodland, whose income should be devoted to the purposes for which they were respectively laid out. In 1731 it was voted to keep school one month in Ebenezer Barker's house, one month in Thomas Eaton's house and a month at Joshua Swan's. In 1733 we find that Ebenezer Barker, Zebediah Barker and Thomas Eaton were each paid £2 10s. for keeping school. In 1735 the town voted to build a school-house eighteen by twenty feet near the meeting-house, school to be kept two months at the school-house and one month at Spicket Hill. The school appears to have been kept at the school-house part of the time, but chiefly at private houses until 1792. Reading and writing and little arithmetic were the principal branch taught, and the latter study was not required. The schools appear to have been taught by male teachers only until 1749, when it voted "to choose school-mistresses to instruct children in their reading." Also voted "to choose James How, Nathaniel Messer, James Ordway and Ebenezer Hibbard a committee to agree with school-mistresses and appoint convenient places for them to be kept in . . ."In 1775, the town was divided into seven school districts, each of which was to have its proportions of the school money, provided it built a comfortable school-house. It appears from the return made to by the committee whose duty it was to build the school-houses, that the building of them was let out at auction to the lowest bidder, and that the houses cost about £29 each. The town also appropriated in the same year £30 for schools, and continued to appropriate that amount each year until 1792. £60 a year was afterwards appropriated for three years, or until 1795, when the first mention of "dollars" appears in the town records. A pound at that time appears to have been equivalent to $3.33. In 1797, $300 was appropriated, and the amount was increased from time to time, until in 1823 the sum appropriated for schools was $600. From that time to the present the increase in the annual school appropriation has more than kept pace with the growth in population until the present year, when the amount appropriated for school purposes was about $11,000.

Up to the year 1775 the selectmen seem to have had usually the sole care of the schools, and from that time to 1798 there was no school committee regularly chosen. It was considered a part of the minister's duty to visit the schools and look after the moral instruction, which in those days formed an important part of the training, as well as to see that the literary instruction did not fall below the proper standard. But in 1798 the town chose a committee of one from each school district, "to inspect the schools in the town, the present year." This way of managing the schools seems to have been followed until 1804, when a committee of three was chosen by the town from each of the nine school districts, making twenty-seven in all. It was also voted "that each committee with the minister visit their respective schools." There seems to have been about this time an unusual interest taken in school matters, for we find among the records of 1800, a system of School Regulations adopted by the town, which show what the duties of School Committees and teachers were then supposed to be, as follows:

Section I.

Concerning the duty of the School Committee.

Act 1. It shall be the duty of the school committee to visit the several town schools, in each district twice every year and more if necessary, giving seasonable notice to the Master or Mistress.

Act 2. It shall be the duty of the Committee to inquire into the regulations, the mode of government, and the method of instruction practiced in the school, and it shall be the duty of the committee to use their best endeavors to correct any deficiency in the mode of government, the manner of instruction, or the discipline of the schools.

Act 3. Should any Master or Mistress appear so essentially deficient in the mode of government, the method of instruction, or the discipline of the school as not to be useful, it shall be the duty of the Committee and Selectmen, a majority of them concurring, to dismiss him or her from the school and the Committee of the Selectmen shall provide another who may be more useful.

Act 4. It shall be the duty of the Committee to close each visit to the school with addressing themselves to the Scholars upon the duty of order, the necessity, respectability, and advantages of good education.

Section II

Concerning the duty of School Masters.

Act 1. It shall be the duty of every School Master to open his school in the morning, and close it in the evening with prayer.

Act 2. It shall be the duty of the Master or Mistress to adopt such general regulations as will have a tendency to operate uniformly throughout the whole school, that every one may have an equal chance to pursue and improve in his particular brand of study and be subject to the same rules of government.

Act 3. The instructor shall endeavor to govern his respective school by the skillfulness of his hand, and the integrity of his heart, with using as little severity as he shall judge will be for the best good of the school, but when mild measures will not subject the idle to the good order and regulations of the school the instructor shall have a right to inflict reasonable and decent corporal punishment.

The system of management above outlined continued until 1822, when the town adopted the plan usually followed throughout the State until the abolishment of the School District system, in 1869. This consisted of a superintending school committee of three, chosen by the town, to look after the qualifications of teachers and the management of the schools, and a prudential committee chosen by the district to hire the teachers, furnish supplies and manage the finances.

The school districts were abolished by statute in 1869. In the winter of the year the High School was organized, and has since been in successful operation. There are eighteen schools in town besides the High School; all kept open nine months in the year.

CHURCHES.

The fact that strikes one most forcibly in reading over the early town records is the prominence given to religious observances. The chief and only reason given for setting off the new town was that the people might more easily attend the public worship of God. The first business done was to provide themselves a minister and a place of public worship. The principal money tax was for the support of these objects. Nothing could show more plainly that the hardy pioneers of Methuen were of genuine Puritan stock. Whatever we may think of Puritan austerity and fanaticism and intolerance, we cannot help admitting the indomitable energy, the iron will and lofty purpose of those men who braved the dangers of hostile Indians and suffered the privations of the wilderness, that they might worship God in their own way.

The old papers which have been preserved, the town records, and the old traditions all show that the first settlers in Methuen were men of rugged, vigorous intellect, accustomed to think for themselves, and not afraid to express their opinions.

The early history of the town was almost identical with the history of the church and society for many years. We have already related some of the incidents connected with the building of the meeting-house and settlement of a pastor, and it remains to give some account of the organization and history of the church since.

From the "Church Records," which were kept by Rev. Christopher Sargent during his ministry, we find that "the first church in Methuen was founded by Rev. Samuel Phillips, of Andover, October 29, 1729." On that day a fast, preparatory to the ordination of Mr. Sargent was kept, a sermon was preached, Rev. Mr. Phillips gathered the church, and the covenant was consented to by twenty-four persons, and within a month thirty-five others joined.

A week afterwards, Rev. Mr. Sargent was ordained pastor, and continued in the pastoral office until 1783, when the town consented to release him from the active duties of the ministry. Mr. Sargent was born in Amesbury, Mass., in 1704 and graduated from Harvard College in 1725. Although he must have had a large influence in the molding the religious and intellectual character of the people of Methuen, there is now very little to be found to show exactly a man of strong common sense, good talents, a moderate man, and one who could unite and harmonize the church. We should also infer that he was a more broad-minded man than the average Congregational minister of his day, from the fact that he was several times called upon by some of his hearers to defend his orthodoxy, and that his Calvinism was not extreme enough to suit them. The church prospered under his ministrations, and during his pastorate, five hundred and nine members were received into it. He died March 20, 1790, and was buried in the old grave-yard on Meeting-House Hill, close to the church here he had ministered for so long. One of his sons, born in Methuen, Nathaniel Peaslee Sargent, became a prominent lawyer, and in 1790, was appointed chief justice of the Supreme Judicial Court of Massachusetts. The only evidence we find in church or town records of serious trouble in the church during Mr. Sargent's long ministry of fifty-three years, was in 1766, when the "Second Church in Methuen" was formed. Thus church was composed of those persons, who to use their own language, "were dissatisfied with the Rev. Mr. Sargent's doctrine and manner of discipline or church government." The records show that church meetings for business were frequent during these times, the discipline strict, and the members closely looked after. It must be admitted, however, judging from some of the entries, that there was need of vigilance, and even then, that sin was not always prevented.

After the retirement of Mr. Sargent it was nearly five years before another minister was settled.

The next pastor was Simon Finley Williams, of Windham, N.H., who was ordained December 13, 1786. He was dismissed in 1791, under suspicion of misconduct. The next pastor was Humphrey C. Perley, of Boxford, who was ordained December 2, 1795. The church was not prosperous during his ministry, although he was a man of good repute, and continued in the pastoral office until May 24, 1815, when he was dismissed at his own request.

Jacob Weed Eastman, of Sandwich, N.H., was the next pastor, was ordained December 13, 1815, and remained until July 4, 1828. He was succeeded by Spencer F. Beard, of West Brookfield, who was installed January 21, 1829, and dismissed April 29, 1832.

He was followed by Sylvester G. Pierce, of Wilmington, Vt. who was installed June 27, 1832, and continued in the pastoral office, greatly beloved by his people, until his death, May 8, 1839. John Charles Phillips, of Boston was installed as the next pastor December 25, 1839.

He was a broad-minded and cultured man, of fine talents, and his pastorate was characterized by peace and harmony in the church. On account of failing health he resigned, in July 1860, and gave up active work in the ministry. Edward H. Greely, of Hopkinton, N.H., was the next pastor, and was installed over the church in 1861, and dismissed in September

1866. The next pastor was Thomas G. Grassie, born in Scotland, and installed in Methuen, September 10, 1867. He was dismissed August 7, 1873. Lyman H. Blake of Cornwall, Vt., was settled in Methuen, June 25, 1874, and was dismissed September 4, 1877. Zephaniah S. Holbrook, of Berea Oh. was the next pastor. He was installed December 4, 1878, and dismissed June 28, 1881. He was succeeded by Joseph Henry Selden, of Hadlyme, Conn. who settled May 10, 1882, and dismissed May 16, 1884. Charles H. Oliphant of Boston, the present pastor, was settled October 29, 1885, having acted as pastor of the church for a year previous to his installation.

The church now numbers about two hundred and fifty members.

In 1796, the old "athadoxt" meeting-house, first built, was torn down, and a new one built on or near the same spot, the congregation worshipping in the meanwhile in the house of the Second Parish. The building of this house seems to have excited much interest through the town, and it is a curious fact, illustrating the habits of the time, that it was voted "That the spectators be given a drink of grog apiece at the rising." As the village sprung up around Spicket Falls, "Meeting-House Hill" ceased to be the most central place, and to better accommodate the congregation, it was decided in 1832, to remove the house to the spot now occupied by the stone meeting-house. It stood there until 1855, when the wooden house was torn down and the present stone house erected. In 1880 the parish received generous contributions from the family of Rev. John C. Phillips, and also from the family of Mr. David Nevins for the purpose of erecting a chapel. The stone chapel now on the grounds was built shortly after. The grounds have since been tastefully laid out and adorned by Henry C, Nevins, Esq., and the church property of the First Parish, Methuen, is now unsurpassed in beauty by any in the Country.

In 1766, April 16, a second church was organized, and Rev. Eliphaz Chapman was installed as its pastor in November 1772.

About this time the "Second Parish" was formed by act of the Legislature. Under this arrangement every taxable person in town was taxed for the support of the minister, but be paid to the parish to which he belonged, instead of to the town. The meeting-house of the Second Parish stood on the north side of Pelham Street, a little west of the house formerly occupied by Leonard Wheeler. It was afterwards removed to the hill, near the house of Stephen W, Williams, whence it was removed to Lawrence, and afterwards destroyed by fire. We have found no record of the termination of the ministry of Mr. Chapman, but we find that Rev. J. H. Stevens was ordained May 18, 1791 and was dismissed March 10, 1795. Rev. Josiah Hill was settled April 9, 1832, and retired April 9, 1833. The Second Parish existed for half a century, until 1816, when it was again united with the old church and parish. At present there is but one Congregational Church in town.

The next church in point of age is the Baptist. To an historical discourse prepared by Rev. K. S. Hall, and delivered at the semi-centennial celebration of that church and society, October 18, 1865, we are indebted for much if what follows. For many years there had been persons of the Baptist faith scattered throughout the town, and Isaac Backus preached here as early as March 30, 1756. It is also known that Baptist sentiments were held by the Messer family in Methuen a century and a half ago, and that Jacob Whittier, of Methuen, was chosen one of the deacons of the Baptist Church in Haverhill May 9, 1765. Sometime during the last century, a Baptist Church was constituted in the west part of Methuen, but no record is in existence of its formation of subsequent proceedings. A meeting-house was built about the year 1778, near the burying-ground west of the Bartlett Farm, and simply boarded and supplied with a floor. Services were held in it occasionally for some years, but some of the leading families removed from town, and the church ceased to exist. Religious meetings continued to be held occasionally at private houses and baptisms were administered at different times, until the formation of the Baptist Society in

Methuen, March 1, 1815, when a number of the inhabitants met at the house of "Mr. Ebenezer Whittier, inn holder," and chose a committee to draft articles of signature, which were signed by seventy-one members during the first year. The Baptist Church was constituted March 8, 1815, and the recognition services were held in the house of Daniel Frye, now the "Butter's Place." During the first year of its organization the church held religious meetings in different parts of the town, the church meetings being usually held at the house of Daniel Frye, afterwards chosen deacon. Charles O. Kimball, a licentiate of the Haverhill Church, commenced preaching June 25, 1815, and was ordained pastor of the church and society May 8, 1816.

In the summer of 1815, steps were taken for building a meeting-house, and it was finally voted to build a "two-story meeting-house" on a half-acre lot given by Bailey Davis, where the Baptist Church now stands. Several other lots were contemplated on which to build the house; one, the "mill lot," embracing a quarter of an acre near where the Town House now stands, and another on "Liberty Hill," a little southwest of the stone church on the opposite side of the street. The house was built and publicly dedicated December 5, 1816. During the long pastorate of Mr. Kimball, the church seems to have been characterized by activity and zeal in its membership, and steadily increased in numbers and influence. For the first ten years all moneys for the support of preaching and other expenses connected therewith were raised by voluntary subscription; afterwards taxes were assessed on members of the society. Mr. Kimball closed his labors October 4, 1835. Rev. Addison Parker, of Sturbridge, was the successor of Mr. Kimball, and was publicly installed February 3, 1836. The church seems to have prospered during his ministry, which closed May 1, 1839. Rev. Samuel W. Field was the next pastor, and was installed April 22, 1840. During the first year of his pastorate, the old meeting-house was torn down and a new one built on the old site, the congregation holding services in the Congregational

Meeting-House until their vestry was ready for use. Mr. Field resigned August 2, 1846.

In June 1847, Rev. Joseph M. Graves became pastor of the church, and remained until May 11, 1850, when he tendered his resignation. Rev. B. F. Bronson was the successor of Mr. Graves, and after a prosperous pastorate of seven years and a half, resigned May 30, 1858.

Rev. Howard M. Emerson was ordained pastor January 2, 1861, and continued in the office until his death, May 18, 1862. Rev. King S. Hall was installed December 23 of the same year, and resigned April 30, 1867. He was succeeded by Rev. N. M. Williams, who was settled February 13, 1868, and left March 31, 1871.

Rev. Lyman Chase became pastor in May 1971, and remained until the summer of 1876. He was succeeded by Rev. Thomas J. B. House, who commenced his labors January 1, 1877, and left April 24, 1883. Rev. Simeon L. B. Chase became the next pastor August 19, 1883, and resigned May 29, 1887.

On Sunday, March 21, 1869, the meeting-house took fire during the morning service, and was totally destroyed. The society erected the house, which is now standing in the following summer on the old spot, and it was dedicated January 13, 1870. This church is strong and prosperous, numbers about two hundred members, and is the only one of its denomination in the town.

The Universalist Church and Society was organized in 1824. At first religious services were held at irregular intervals in the different school-houses in town. As the church became stronger, meetings were held regularly in "McKay's building," on Lowell Street, and later in "Wilson's Hall," Hampshire Street. The present Universalist meeting-house was built 1835-36, and dedicated in July, 1836. Rev. John A Gurley was the first settled minister, and was pastor at that time. He left about 1837. The next pastor was Rev. E. N. Harris, who did not remain long.

Rev. A. A. Miner was settled over the church in November 1839, and remained until July 1842, when he left to settle in Lowell. Rev. H. R. Nye was the next pastor, and remained about three years, leaving in 1845. Rev. William Spaulding succeeded Mr. Nye, and preached at this time two or three years. Rev. O. A. Tillotson succeeded Mr. Spaulding, and was followed by Rev. William Waggoner in 1851 and 1852. Mr. Willard Spaulding was pastor for a second time in 1855 and 1856. Rev. Edwin Davis became pastor in the spring of 1861, and remained until 1863. Rev. John E. Davenport followed Mr. Davis, and continued in the pastoral office about two years. Rev. C. A. Bradley became pastor in 1869, and resigned March 22, 1871.

During the pastorate of Mr. Bradley, the church and grounds were remodeled and much improved. Rev. W. W. Heywood became pastor in 1871, and his resignation was accepted by the society March 29, 1875. Rev. R. T. Polk was installed as the next pastor March 21, 1877, and resigned August 31, 1879.

Rev. G. T. Flanders, of Lowell, supplied the pulpit for a year, beginning his labors February 29, 1880, was succeeded by Rev. Nathan S. Hill from November 1, 1881, to March 1, 1883. In October, 1883, the society called Rev. Donald Fraser to the pastorate, and he remained until his resignation in November 1885. Rev. A. F. Walch, the next minister, was installed October 14, 1886, and is now in the pastoral office. The congregation numbers about one hundred and fifty.

We are informed that the Methodists first held meetings in Methuen in 1833 or '34. They occasionally occupied the Second Parish meeting-house, and held meetings in the school-houses, but after the institution of regular religious services, they occupied "Wilson's Hall." The building now used as a school house on Lowell Street, was built by them for a meeting-house, and occupied for several years, until the establishment of a Methodist Church and society at the new city of Lawrence drew off a portion of the members, and so weakened the society in Methuen that it was thought advisable to sell the building. After the sale of the meeting-house no regular religious services were held in Methuen by that denomination until 1853 or 1854, when a reorganization was effected, and religious services were held in the library room in the town hall. As the society increased in numbers, more commodious quarters were needed, and the society held their meetings in the town hall until 1871, when the present meeting-house was built at the junction of Lowell and Pelham Streets. John Barnes of Lawrence was the first pastor after the reorganization, and since then the pastors have been as follows:

Rev. Charles Young, from June 1867 to April 1857.

Rev. Elijah Mason, from April 1857 to April 1858.

Rev. Nathaniel L. Chase, from April 1858 to May 1859.

Rev. John L. Trefren, from May 1859 to April 1861

Rev. Charles R. Harding, from April 1961 to April 1862.

Rev. Joshua B. Horman, from April 1862 to April 1864.

Rev. William Hewes, from April 1864 to April 1865.

Rev. Nelson Green, from April 1865 to April 1866.

Rev. Larnard L. Eastman, from April 1866 to April 1869.

Rev. James Noyes, from April 1869 to April 1872.

Rev. George I. Judkins from April 1873 to April 1875.

Rev. Charles A. Cressy, from April 1875 to April 1877.

Rev. S. C. Farnham, from April 1877 to April 1879.

Rev. J. W. Walker from April 1879 to April 1881.

Rev. O. W. Baketel, from April, 1881 to April 1884.

Rev. H. H. French from April 1884 to April 1886.

Rev. Alexander McGregor, from April 1886.

The church numbers one hundred and thirty-two members.

In 1833, or thereabouts, there was an Episcopal Church formed in Methuen. It seems to have had a short existence as an organized body, and little can be learned about it, except that it held its meetings in "Wilson's Hall." In 1878, another Episcopal Church was organized under the name of St. Thomas'

Church, and a church-building erected on Broadway near Lawrence line. The membership is largely composed of residents of Lawrence.

The first rector was Rev. Belno A. Brown, whose energy and zeal contributed much to the success of the new church. The present rector is Rev. Thomas De Learsy.

The Catholics have a large and prosperous branch of that church in Methuen. For many years there have been a large number of persons in the town, holding that faith, who attended church in Lawrence. In January, 1878, a movement was made by leading Catholics in Methuen, and approved by Father Gilmore, then Parish Priest in Lawrence, to establish religious services. The Town Hall was engaged, and has been occupied for that purpose on Sundays ever since. Father Marsden officiated from the beginning until his death nearly two years afterwards.

The pastors who succeeded him have been Father O'Farrell, about one year; Father Riley, about two years; Father O'Connell, about two years; Father Rowan about two years; and Father Murphy, who is the present pastor. The congregation numbers about four hundred persons.

ORGANIZATIONS.

Methuen has had her full share of social and charitable organizations.

Grecian Lodge, F.A.A.M., was formed in Methuen December 14, 1825, and seems to have prospered until the Anti-Masonic excitement overspread the country. In consequence of this surrendered its charter in 1838. The lodge reorganized in 1847 under the old charter, but within the limits of Lawrence. Methuen Masons associated themselves with the old lodge until 1860, when John Hancock Lodge was constituted. It holds its meetings in "Currier's Building," where it has a cozy, well-furnished lodge-room, and numbers about one-hundred and fifty members.

Hope Lodge of Odd Fellows was instituted in 1844, and for a time held its meetings in "Currier's Building." It surrendered its charter to the Grand Lodge in 1855. The lodge was reinstated in 1869, and since that time, has flourished. It has pleasant rooms, well-furnished, in Dodge's Building, and numbers about one hundred and forty members.

A branch of the Royal Arcanum was established here in December, 1877. It commenced with a membership of twenty, and now has eighty-five. It holds its meetings in Corliss' Hall, and seems to be a prosperous society—if we can call an Insurance Association of that size prosperous, which has had only one death among its members for ten years.

The United Order of the Pilgrim Fathers also have a strong organization in Methuen. It was formed March 15, 1879, and numbers about one hundred members. They hold their meetings in the hall of the Grand Army of the Republic.

Wm. B. Green Post 100, Grand Army of the Republic, was organized in February 1877, and has seventy-four members. It has one of the finest Grand Army halls in the region, tastefully finished and elegantly furnished. As the Grand Army is composed only of veterans in the late war, the post cannot expect to increase much in numbers, but the zeal and interest of its members seem in no ways to diminish as time goes on.

In 1873, Minerva Lodge, Daughters of Rebecca, I. O. of O. F., was instituted. It numbers about ninety members.

The "Home Circle" number about fifty members was organized in May 1880. They hold their meetings in the hall of the Grand Army of the Republic.

A branch of the "United Order of Workmen" was organized January 25, 1886, and has thirty-one members. They meet in the hall of the G. A. R.

The Knights of Labor have a strong and well-organized association in Methuen, and hold their meetings in Corliss's Hall.

METHUEN LYCEUM.

Methuen does not appear to have been behind other towns of like population and wealth in efforts for literary culture and entertainment. About 1819 a society was formed called the "Addison Literary Society," for purposes of mental culture and improvement. We have been informed by Robert S. Rantoul, Esq. of Salem, that two or three years after, principally through the efforts of Timothy Claxton, and English Mechanic and Machinist in the cotton mill, this society was transformed into what was afterwards known as a lyceum. And there is some reason to suppose that this was the beginning of the "lyceum" in this country. This society flourished nearly or quite twenty years, had a small library and erected a building in which to hold meetings on Broadway near Park Street. But after a while, a sinful desire for dramatic entertainment entered into the minds of some of its members, and the acting of farces and short plays to some extent took the place of the sober discussions of great questions, which formed the staple of the earlier exercises. The sober, substantial people of the town looked on more in sorrow than in anger, and refused to countenance such loose and immoral practices. From this time on the society declined and fell, and utter ruin overtook it with the performance of *Richard III* by some of its members.

The building was sold and removed to the west side of the river and converted unto a dwelling house now owned and occupied by Hon. James O. Parker. For many years, courses of lectures were given almost every winter, and sometimes a debating club was organized, until the easy access to Lawrence made it possible for Methuen people to attend entertainments there almost as easily as at home.

NEVINS MEMORIAL LIBRARY.

In 1873, and every year thereafter until 1887, the town voted that the proceeds received from dog licenses should be devoted to the purchase of a public library. From this small beginning the number of volumes increased year by year until in 1886 a library of about twenty-five hundred well selected volumes was collected, which was much used by the people of the town, until the Nevins Memorial Library was opened to the public—January 1, 1887.

There is nothing in Methuen in which the citizens take so much pride, and which they are so grateful, as the Nevins Memorial. The design of this institution is so well stated in the "Note by the Trustee," published in the catalog of the library that we quote it entire:

The Nevins Memorial was founded in memory of the late David Nevins, who was born in Salem, N.H., Dec. 12, 1809, and was brought to Methuen by his parents at an early age, and passed here the years of his childhood. In his later years, he assumed the duties of a citizen, and here at the family homestead he was seized with the illness, which, on the 19th of March 1881, unexpectedly closed his active and useful career.

Desiring to promote the intellectual and moral well-being of the community whose material interests had been so greatly advanced by his business sagacity and energy, it was his expressed intention to found, during his lifetime, an institution similar in scope to that of this Memorial. His sudden decease prevented his execution of this design, but the purpose he had declared was at once taken up by his widow and sons, and the Nevins Memorial Building was erected upon the site chosen and purchased for that use some years before his death. The building was planned, and its construction supervised, by Mr. Samuel J. F. Thayer, architect, of Boston; ground for its erection being broken March 27, 1883, and the completed structure first opened to the public June 11, 1884. It contains a public hall, ample in size and beautiful in decoration, a library, waiting and reading rooms well adapted to their respective uses, and suitable rooms for the trustees and librarian. The government of the Memorial is vested in a board of seven trustees, five of whom, Mrs. Eliza S. Nevins and Messrs. David Nevins, Henry C. Nevins, Jacob Emerson, and John H. Morse, were incorporated by the Massachusetts legislature of 1885 as permanent members. The two additional members are chosen by the town of Methuen for the term of two years, Dr. George E. Woodbury and James Ingalls, are the presented elective members.

When experience shall have shown what amount is needed for the proper maintenance of the Memorial, it is the design of the founders to make an endowment sufficient to render it entirely self-supporting. The library comprises nearly ten thousand volumes of standard works, carefully selected, and covering a wide range of general literature and special topics. To Miss Ames was entrusted its entire organization, including the selection of the books, the details of classification and arrangement, and the preparation of the catalogue. We feel confident that the result of her labors will not only facilitate the use of the library for general readers, but also will be found of particular advantage to those pursuing a systematic course of reading, or engaged in special studies. The end crowns the work.

The building is of brick, with freestone trimmings, of beautiful architectural design, and built in the most substantial manner. Every foundation wall and pier rests upon the solid rock, and the walls are exceptionally strong and heavy,

The building is finished in oak throughout, and all the ornamentation, within and without, is in the most exquisite taste. No expense was spared to make it a perfect work, according to the designs of the founders. The library, selected and arranged by Miss Harriet H. Ames, is admirably and prepared by her, is a well nigh prefect specimen of the art of cataloging. It is in two volumes, of nearly five hundred pages each, and is an encyclopedia in itself. The following inscription on the front of the building explains the purpose of the founders:

This Hall and Library
erected and endowed by
Eliza S. Nevins, his widow
and by David and Henry C
Nevins, his children
is a memorial of
David Nevins
Born 1809. Died 1881.

About three and a half acres of land surrounding the building have been set apart and tastefully laid out and ornamented with rare trees and shrubs. And all this beautiful and costly estate is placed in the hands of trustees, and is to be endowed with a fund to make it self-supporting, for the benefit of the inhabitants of Methuen in all coming time. Surely, no more noble or lasting tribute could have been paid to the memory of a beloved husband and father, and no benevolence could have been made wider in its scope or more far-reaching in its influence. Then intellectual growth and culture resulting from the use of this library and reading-room will only begin to be seen in this generation; the best results can never be known to those who have established this noble beneficence.

The beautiful and well-kept grounds will be an educator of no small influence, and many a home will be made pleasanter and more attractive from the example there perpetually shown.

The interest already manifested by the young people of the town in the use of the library, and the average high character of the books most sought for, must be to the generous founders a most pleasing feature of the opening of the library to the public.

NEWSPAPERS.

The first newspaper published in Methuen was *the Iris*, which was removed here from Haverhill in 1833. It was supposed to have been printed as a campaign paper in the interest of Caleb Cushing, and was soon discontinued. The next newspaper was *the Methuen Falls Gazette*, which was first issued January 3, 1835, by S. Jameson Varney. It was "neutral in politics" and not published many years.

The Methuen Transcript and Essex Farmer was established in 1876 by C. L. Houghton & Co., and edited by Charles E. Trow, who soon after became its proprietor, and continued to edit the paper until it passed into the hands of Fred A. Lowell,

Esq. its present editor and publisher. It is a weekly paper of excellent moral tone, published every Friday, and the only newspaper now published in Methuen.

The Methuen Enterprise was established by Daniel A. Rollins, March 6, 1880, and published by him till his death, March 25, 1882, and was a bright, readable, spicy sheet.

After his death, it was purchased by Sellers Bros., and published by them until September 1883, when it was merged in *the Lawrence Eagle*.

FIRE DEPARTMENT.

In 1826 or '27, a small fire-engine, the "Tiger," was bought, one-half the cost being paid by the Methuen Company, and the other half by Major Osgood, John Davis, Thomas Thaxter, George A. Waldo and J. W. Carleton. Thomas Thaxter was the first foreman. There is no evidence that the town had any concern in its management. This was the only protection against fire until 1846, when the selectmen were authorized to purchase a new fire-engine and hose, and erect a house. This engine (The Spiggot) was manned by an active and efficient company, and did good service till 1870, when the steamer "E. A. Straw," was purchased and the Spiggot laid aside.

Methuen now has an excellent fire department, the E. A. Straw Company of seventeen men, and the Mystic Hose Company of ten men, organized in 1878, all well trained and efficient.

In addition to this there are iron pipes laid through the principal streets, and connected with the powerful engines of the Methuen Company, through which water can be forced, over the principal portion of the village, in case of fire.

CEMETERIES.

One of the first things done by the old settlers was to lay out a place to bury their dead. In 1828, the town voted "that there should be a graveyard provided by the town, somewhere near the meeting-house," and chose William Whittier and Joshua Swan to measure and bound out the said graveyard.

Their report to the town describes the lot as follows: "Beginning with a small pine tree marked with the letter B, thence running southerly to a pine stump marked with B, twenty rods in length; thence to a pine tree marked with a B, a northeasterly about six or seven rods in width, and so to another pine tree marked with a B, northwesterly about twenty rods, and so to the bounds first mentioned." This was undoubtedly the north end of the "old burying-ground" on Meeting-House Hill. In 1803, it was enlarged "on the south side," and a hearse was purchased "for the more convenient solemnization of funerals."

In 1772, the Selectmen were ordered to lay out a burying-ground in the west part of the town. They laid out one-fourth of an acre, on land given for the purpose by Richard Whittier. The lot was afterwards enlarged, and as the ground became occupied, it was again enlarged in 1876.

The burial-ground on Lawrence Street was purchased and laid out about 1830.

The three burial-places comprised those owned by the town, and are now but little used.

Walnut Grove Cemetery was laid out by an association of individuals, in 1853. It is situated on the high and overlooking the village on the west side, and is a place of much natural beauty, which has been greatly increased by tasteful arrangement of the grounds, and beautiful memorials erected to the dead.

BUSINESS.

The Town of Methuen was at first almost exclusively an agricultural community. Still there is reason to believe that there was a variety of occupations in the town at an early day. There are traditions of coopers, tanners, hatters, shoemakers, morocco-dressers, and there is mention of "Iron works" on the Spicket, in that part of Methuen now within the limits of Lawrence. Probably there were persons in the town to make almost everything required for use by the inhabitants. There was no village, and at first probably found small market for their products outside of the community immediately around them. The farmers were so far from market that their money incomes must have been very small. They depend on the city of Salem as a market for their produce, and their wood and timber was rafted to Newburyport. Hemp and flax perhaps found a market to some extent in Londonderry.

These places were the only outlets of importance for their surplus products, until after the city of Lowell was founded, when everything, except wood, was carried there, and the farmers found the new market greatly for their advantage. Lowell continued to be the principal market for agricultural products, until the building of Lawrence furnished a more convenient and, in some respects, better market than Lowell, and gave the farmers of Methuen as good facilities for the successful cultivation of the land as can be found in any part of New England. Nevertheless, it is a curious fact that the population of Methuen, outside of the village, is no larger now than at the beginning of the Revolutionary War. It is even doubtful if there is a much greater acreage of cleared land now than at that time. It is not to be supposed, however, that there are no more farmers now than then, or that the value of the agriculture if the town is no greater than is entirely changed, and the product of a single acre new frequently has a greater value than the entire crop of a large farm in the olden time.

From the old traditions, we should judge that the manufacture of hats has been carried on in Methuen from a very early date. There are several places pointed out in the east part of the town, as the site of ancient hatter's shops. The work was done entirely by hand, no doubt in a small way at first, and half a dozen men or less could carry on the whole business of a shop. Within the memory of many hatters now living, the manufacture was done entirely in this way. But, with the introduction of machinery, the business has been concentrated into a few factories, by which the production has largely increased. Nearly all the hats now made in the town, are manufactured at the factories of James Ingalls and J. Milton Tenney.

A similar statement would perhaps be true of the shoe business, which for many years has been an important industry in Methuen. In the early days, shoe-making was not carried on to so great an extent as hatting. But within the recollection of many now living, there was a shoemaker's shop in every neighborhood and at almost every house.

Shoes were all made by hand, and the workmen took out all the stock, all cut, from the shop of their employer, and carried it home to make up. In those days to be, a shoemaker was to know how to make an entire shoe. Farmers' and shoemakers' wives and daughters "bound" shoes, and the board of the shoemakers formed an important part of the income in many families. It would have been hard to find a spot in Methuen, where in the still summer days, the sound of the shoemaker's hammer did not penetrate. But after the war came on, and labor became scarce, machinery was devised to do the work, which had been performed by hand, and the business began to center into factories, like hatting, where, by the use of machinery, the production is largely increased.

In past times, it is dependent on the shoe business for a live-lihood, than on the manufacturer of hats. At present the shoe factory of Tenney & Co., is the only one in operation in Methuen.

The first store in town was opened by Abial Howe, at a build-ing on Howe Street, nearly opposite the house of Charles L. Tozier. The exact date is unknown, but it is within the recollec-tion of persons now living. Later, Esquire Russ opened an-other store a little south of the Russ place, but it does not ap-pear that either of them had an extensive business.

WATER POWER.

It is not known precisely when Spicket Falls was first utilized as a water-power. A deed is in existence from the widow of John Morrill, dated December 1709, in which she conveys to Rob-ert Swan, for the sum of thirty pounds, one-fourth of a sawmill and land, "on Spicket River Falls, the mill that was built by and belonged to and amongst Robert Swan, John Morrill and Elisha Davis." Without doubt, this was the first mill built. Afterwards a grist-mill was built on each side of the river, and as there was not business enough to keep them both running, it was agreed between them that they should run on alternate weeks. This arrangement was kept up until the cotton factory was built. The first cotton factory was built somewhere near 1812, by Stephen Minot, Esq. of Haverhill, on the north side of the river. This was burned in 1818, and soon after rebuilt. In July 1821, the whole privilege and lands connected therewith were purchased by the Methuen Company. The old carding of fulling-mill, which had stood on the south side of the Falls, was moved away and converted into a dwelling-house, which now stands on the north side of Pelham Street. In 1826-27, the brick mill was built as it now stands. In 1864, the property came into the possession of David Nevins, Esq., by whom it was largely increased in capac-ity and value, and to whose enterprise the town is greatly in-

80

debted for its prosperity in recent years. He erected a large addition to the brick mill, and introduced the manufacture of jute, which was continued until his death, in 1881. The mill has since been kept in operation by his family. The principal manufacture of the Methuen Company has been cotton goods. "Methuen Duck" has been for many years a well-known article in the market, and "Methuen ticking" has always been a principal article of manufacture. After the death of Mr. Nevins, the jute machinery was removed, and in addition to duck and ticking, the Methuen Company now manufactures awning material and light and heavy cotton flannels.

In 1824, a saw-mill and grist-mill were built where the Methuen woolen-mill stands. They came into the procession of Samuel A. Harvey, Esq., by whom the business of the respective mills was carried on for some years. In 1864, the Methuen Woolen Company bought out the privilege, and erected a factory where the manufacture of woolen goods has been since carried on. The Arlington Mills have a large factory in Methuen, near the Lawrence line, built in 1881, devoted to the manufacturer of fine cotton yarn. The other mills of this enterprising and prosperous corporation are situated a little below on the Spicket, but within the limit of Lawrence.

The extensive chemical works of Lee, Blackburn & Co. are also situated in Methuen. They produce commercial fertilizers and chemicals used in manufacturing processes.

The variety of manufacturing interests in the town, the nearness to Lawrence, and close connection by the horse-railroad, which has been in operation since 1867, have combined in times of business depression to prevent that utter stagnation in business, which has been so severely felt in isolated manufacturing towns having only one important industry.

We have thus presented such of the principal features in the history of Methuen, past and present, as space will permit. Many details have been omitted, and some subjects altogether neglected, which would doubtless be of interest to those acquainted with the town, but the limits assigned to this paper will not admit of an exhaustive history.

INDEX.

Bradford 9, 10
Bradley, Rev. C. A. 68
Broadway 50, 70, 72
Bronson, Rev. Benjamin F. 67
Brown, Rev. Belno A. 70
Brown, Silas 38, 41, 46
Butters farm 51
Butter's Place 66
Button, Matthias 18

C

Calton, Ebenezer 38
Campbell, James 41, 46
Cape Ann 13
Carleton, Ebenezer 45
Carleton, Eleazar 41
Carleton, Elijah 44
Carleton, J. W. 76
Carleton, Kimball 44
Carlton, Eben 39
Carlton, Elijah 39
Carlton, Kimball 38
Catholic Church 70
Chapman, Eliphaz 64
Charbourne, Capt. Benjamin F. 53
Charles River 34
Chase, James 38
Chase, Rev. Lyman 67
Chase, Rev. Nathaniel L. 69
Chase, Rev. Simeon L. B. 67
Chellis, Timothy 42, 46
chemical works 81
Cheney, Enoch 43
Clark, Ephraim 26, 27, 38, 44
Clark, Nathaniel 39, 44
Clark, Samuel 26, 27
Claxton, Timothy 72
Clements, Robert 15
Cluff, Jonathan 51
Cobbett's Pond 24
Coffin, Tristan 15
Cole, Samuel 43
Colonial Census 44

Colten, Ebenezer 37
Company B, 14th Massachusetts
    Infantry 53, 54
Concord River 13
Corgill, Robert 27
Corliss, David 46
Corliss, Jonathan 33
Corliss's Hall 72
cotton factory 80
Cressy, Rev. Charles A. 69
Cross, Abiel 39, 44
Cross, John 20, 27, 38
Cross, Joseph 44
Cross, Samuel 43
Cross, Simeon 38, 44
Cross, William 20, 27
Cummings, Henry 53
Currant's Hill 50
currency 50
Currier, Asa 38
Currier, Daniel 53
Currier, Richard 38
Currier, Samuel 27
Currier's Building 70
Cushing, Caleb 75

D

Dale, Surgeon Gen. William 56
Dame, Albert L. 53, 55
Daughters of Rebecca, I. O. of O. F.
    71
Davenport, Rev. John E. 68
Davis, John 42
Davis, Capt. John 45, 46
Davis, Elisha 80
Davis, James 18, 27
Davis, John 39, 76
Davis, John Capt. 41
Davis, Mitchell 43, 46
Davis, Rev. Edwin 68
Davis, Thomas 15
Davison, James 39, 42, 46
Davison, John 38, 45

Hampton Falls 34
Hancock, Gov. John 48
Hancock, John 44
Harding, Rev. Charles R. 69
Harriman, Amos 41, 46
Harris, Peter 42
Harris Pond 10
Harris, Rev. E. N. 67
Harris, John 28
Harris's Ferry 49
Harvey, Samuel A. 81
Haseltine, Nathaniel 38, 44
Hastens, Simeon 38
Hastings, John 27
Hastings, Joseph 38
Hastings, Robert 38
hat shops 79
Haverhill 9, 10, 11, 14, 15, 16,
   17, 19, 21, 22
Hawke's Brook 11
Hawke's Brook 12
Hawke's Meadow Brook 22
Hawke's Meadow Brook 21, 24
Haynes, Jonathan 20
Herrick, Benjamin 42
Herrick, Ebenezer 42, 46, 47
Herrick, Nathaniel 38, 41, 45
Herrick, Thomas 44
Hewes, Rev. William 69
Heywood, Rev. W. W. 68
Hibbard, Ebenezer 58
Hibbard, James 43
Hibbard, John Jr. 43
Hibbard, Joseph 42, 46, 47
Hibbard, Nathaniel 43
Hibbard, William 43
Higginson, Colonel 19
Hill, Josiah 65
Hill, Rev. Nathan S. 68
Holbrook, Zephaniah S. 64
Holt's Rock 15
Hope Lodge of Odd Fellows 71
Horman, Rev. Joshua B. 69

horse-railroad 81
Houghton & Co. 75
Houghton, C. L. 75
House, Rev. Thomas J. B. 67
How, Abiel 38
How, Jacob 39
How, James 26, 27, 58
How, Jonathan 39, 44
How, Joseph 39
How, Rev. Moses 57
How, Timothy 38
Howe, Abial 80
Howe, John Jr. 38
Howe Street 20, 80
Hubbard, Lazarus 46
Hughs, Isaac 42
Hughs, John 43
Hughs, Samuel 43
Huse, John 37, 40, 48
Huse, Samuel 28
Huse, Stephen 32

I

Indian attack 20
Indian relics 13
Indian Ridge 11
Indians 12, 15
Ingalls, James
   40, 42, 46, 50, 57, 74
Ipswich 14
the Iris 75
Island Pond 9

J

Jackson, Joseph 42
Jaques, Richard 38
Jenners, J. K., Mayor of Haverhill
   57
Jennings, Daniel 41
Jennings, Solomon 42, 46
John Hancock Lodge 70
Johnnot, Prince 42
Jones, Amos G. 53

Y